The Pain from the
Death of a Spouse

A Diary of Life, Love, Death, and Sorrow

BUDDY ROGERS

WESTBOW®
PRESS
A DIVISION OF THOMAS NELSON
& ZONDERVAN

Scripture taken from the King James Version of the Bible.

WestBow Press books may be ordered through booksellers or by contacting:

WestBow Press
A Division of Thomas Nelson & Zondervan
1663 Liberty Drive
Bloomington, IN 47403
www.westbowpress.com
1 (866) 928-1240

ISBN: 978-1-4908-5216-4 (sc)
ISBN: 978-1-4908-5217-1 (hc)
ISBN: 978-1-4908-5218-8 (e)

Library of Congress Control Number: 2014916542

Printed in the United States of America.

WestBow Press rev. date: 10/16/2014

CONTENTS

Foreword xi
Preface xiii
Acknowledgements xv
Dedication of Book xvii

CHAPTER 1

Introduction 1
Categories of Death 2
One Remained 3
Wow! What a Beginning! 5
Marriage Is a Learning Experience 6
It's a Baby! 7
I Have a Problem 8
Serious Sickness 9
    Fast-Forward to 2001 9
Pulmonary, Respiratory, and Pseudomonas 10
    Fast-Forward to 2006 10
Heavenly Assurance 12
    Fast-Forward to May 11, 2012 12
Mother's Day 2012 15
    Sunday, May 13, 2012 15
    Monday, May 14, 2012 15
    Tuesday, May 15, 2012 16
The Final Good-Bye 17
    Wednesday, May 16, 2012 17

How Quickly Circumstances Changed My Life 21

CHAPTER 2

Money Can't Buy It...23
Death, Pain, and Alone 29
    Wednesday, May 30, 2012 (two weeks after D-day) 29
    Rewind to February 2012.. 30
A Sympathy Note from Myself to Myself 31
Statements of Sympathy 32
My Opinion of Death Comments 32
    Comments that May Not Be Helpful to the Griever 32
    Comments and Behavior that May Be Helpful to the Griever 34
Remembering..35
Time Alone 36
All Things Work Together for Good..36

CHAPTER 3

Grief Road Maps...39
Levels, Periods, Degrees, and Stages of Grief...............................41
On the Mountaintop and Down in the Valley..............................42
A Pyramid of Daily Grief..43
    Thursday, May 17, 2012 (one day after D-day) 43
    Friday, May 18, 2012 (two days after D-day)................................... 44
    Saturday, May 19, 2012 (three days after D-day) 45
    Sunday, May 20, 2012 (four days after D-day) 45
    Monday, May 21, 2012 (five days after D-day, day of the funeral)....45
    Tuesday, May 22, 2012 (six days after D-day) 47
    Wednesday, May 23, 2012 (seven days after D-day) 48
Why Cry?..49
Emotional Suffering 50
My Death-Pain Comparison 51
Margie and I .... Love and Marriage. 51
Initial Shock about My Spouse's Death 53
    Rewind to May 16 2012 (D-day)...53
A Life of "No Mores" 54
    Saturday, March 16, 2013 (ten months after D-day).................... 56

Ten Things a Lost Person Will Discover, One Second after Death...59

    May 9, 2012 (seven days before Margie's death)................................ 60

    Fast-Forward to August 31, 2012 (three months after D-day).......... 60

Getting Things Done Four Months after D-day.............................61

    September 20, 2012...61

I Married the Girl Next Door 64

CHAPTER 4

One Year after D-Day 65

    May 16, 2013 65

Taking Spouses for Granted 66

Writing My Diary..66

    June 16, 2012 (one month after D-day).. 66

References to Death 67

You Know What I Think I'll Do?...68

A Cedar Chest..71

The Wedding Dress..71

    August 1, 2012 (eleven weeks after D-day) 71

Margie's Personal Things 72

    July 13, 2012 72

    September 22, 2012.. 73

Neutral Ground in a Marriage 73

    Rewind to 1969 73

The Move from Florida to California..74

    Fast-Forward to 1974...74

Loneliness 76

Death Loneliness...76

CHAPTER 5

The Words I Love You..79

Whimpering and Whining to God 80

    September 20, 2012 (four months after D-day) 80

The Pain, Fourteen Months after D-day...81

    Tuesday, July 23, 2013...81

    Saturday, July 27, 2013 81

A Loss May Produce a Gain 82
    Rewind to 1964.. 82
Love Cards between Spouses 84
    September 2012 (three months after D-day)................... 84
    Fast-forward to April 26, 2013 (eleven months after D-day)........... 85
Living Alone 85
Friends and Grieving...86
Every Life has a Story 87
    November 16, 2012 (six months after D-day)................. 87

CHAPTER 6

The Grief Experience...89
Love and Faith 90
Opposites Attract 93
Love of Simple Things 95
Eternity..97
What I'm Thankful for, Thanksgiving 2013 98
The First Days in Fifty-Five Years without My Spouse....................99

CHAPTER 7

Father's Day 2013.. 101
    Sunday, June 16, 2013 101
    Rewind to May 16, 2012, D-day 101
Where Did All The Years Go? 102
Adam and Eve..104
    Rewind to the Beginning of the Human Race............... 104
Kindred Hospital Stay...108
    Fast-forward to December 2011–March 2012 108
Margie and Heaven 109

CHAPTER 8

Once-in-a-Lifetime Vacation 113
If I Had My Life to Live Over.. 117
One-Year Death Anniversary... 118
    May 16, 2013 118
God Is the Answer 118

Where There Is "Blank," Let there be "Blank" 121
Car and Church 122
    Rewind to a Sunday in 1990, Torrance, California........................ 122

Chapter 9

Progression of Sickness 123
    Stages of my Declining Spouse (11/23/2011 - 5/22/2012).............. 123
    November 23, 2011 123
    December 7, 2011 123
    December 15, 2011 124
    December 27, 2011 124
    December 28, 2011 125
    January 3, 2012 125
    January 5, 1012 126
    January 9, 2012 126
    January 27, 2012 127
    January 31, 2012 128
    February 13, 2012 129
    February 16, 2012 129
    February 17, 2012 130
    February 20, 2012 131
    February 25, 2012 131
    March 2, 2012 131
    March 14, 2012 132
    March 21, 2012 132
    March 28, 2012 133
    April 4, 2012 133
    April 28, 2012 134
    May 8, 2012 134
    May 14, 2012 135
    May 15, 2012 135
    May 16, 2012 136
    May 22, 2012 136

Chapter 10

Valentine's Day 2014 137
    Fifty-five Years of Valentines.. 137

The End-of-Life Decisions 140
The End of the Diary 140
    Eighteen Months after D-day 140
Recovery 141
My Six Footprints to Recovery 141
Poem: Margie, the Girl Next Door 143
God's Comfort Zone 148

FOREWORD

God is so good at spoiling His children as He bestows upon us His amazing and abundant gifts each and every day. Each of us need and desire these gifts in order to fulfill God's purpose for our lives. In God's Word we are taught that the greatest of these gifts is the gift of Love! This gift is not to be an optional part of our life that we simply open and use it if we feel like doing so. This gift actually is commanded by God that we use it daily in order that we may be successful in life. The area that we are designed to achieve life's greatest successes is in the relationships of our life. We are to love God with all our heart, soul, and strength. We are to love our neighbors as we love ourselves. We are created, sustained and commanded to love!

I have had the privilege of reading the pages that are to follow and you are in store for a blessing. What you will read is an incredible love story between Buddy and Margie Rogers. Their love for each other through the years conquered the obstacles and challenges of their life together. It is this love that they shared together that Buddy will allow you to see which continues to conquer the challenges Buddy faces through the death of Margie. Buddy will allow you to look into his heart and you will see how love enables us to have a victory in dealing with death, grief, and loneliness. This love story reminds us that we can not prevent or stop the hardships of life from occurring but we do have a choice to how we will deal with these challenges. The author reminds us of what the Author of Life states that "Love Conquers Everything".

Dr. Myles Dowdy
Doctor of Education (Ed. D)
Master of Divinity (M Div.)
Minister of Administration/Counseling
First Baptist Church, Brandon, Florida

Preface

This book introduces a Door that every married couple will walk through, usually not together. A Door that we don't like to acknowledge, or even admit that it exists. It is the Door of reality. One spouse will die before the other in almost every marriage. My spouse walked through the Door and left me on the other side. This is my story after the Door closed behind her.

It's a story that speaks to the soul of mankind about the future in every marriage. Stop for a moment and think about life without your spouse. Don't rush it, give it some though. Then today, you can hug your spouse a little tighter and a little longer as you whisper, *'I love you.'*

The anniversaries of life roll by at an astonishing rate. Appreciate the gift of existence and love for they are a valuable commodity and a precious gem.

This is a book to give to yourself, to your mother, to your father, to your grand mother, to your grand father, to your family and to your friends. Every one of these lives will be changed forever when a spouse dies.

ACKNOWLEDGEMENTS

First, I must thank God for giving me the expressions, the phrases and the words to write this book. He stood with me as I felt **The Pain from the Death of a Spouse**. He stood close enough to be touched as I wrote the words of Life, Love, Death and Sorrow. I could not have completed this book without God's guidance, support and assistance.

I would like to express a special thanks to Dr. Myles Dowdy for accepting the challenge to read and re-read this manuscript. Also giving comfort and advice; cheering me on; and providing empathy when needed. Many thanks for writing the Foreword to this book.

I would like to thank Naomi Kline for assuming the task of locating my incorrect characteristics of the English language. Thank you for finding my errors and correcting them, yet I continued making errors after you completed your mission. You may be able to teach old dogs new tricks but most old dogs cannot remember what they were taught. I accept the reality of being human: *Any wording errors or inaccuracies in this book are the fault of the author.*

I would like to thank Bill and Linda Clark who have been loving friends for many years. Thank you for your encouragement and devotion during the writing of this book. Also, thank you for your continued love that you have given Margie and me over the years.

I would like to thank Pat and Garney Williams for their friendship for more than fifty years. Thank you for your support during the writing of this book.

There are others, too numerous to name, who have given comfort and aid. I owe them all a debt of gratitude for helping me look beyond ..
The Pain from the Death of a Spouse.

And lastly, I thank my departed spouse, Margie, because without her warm and compassionate love, I would not have an actuality to write about.

DEDICATION OF BOOK

With Love, Gratitude and Delight I dedicate this Book:

To Our Son, Ed and his family

To Our Daughter, Wendy and her family

In Honor of their Mother

CHAPTER 1

Introduction

May these suggestions encourage you to give more time and affection to your loved ones, especially your spouse and your children? My greatest human loss has been the death of my spouse. Each of my family members' death carried its own individual and personal pain, but my supreme pain came from the death of Margie. Her death defines what matters in life, love and marriage, and what doesn't. Her love of fifty-five years continues to imprison my heart, body, and soul. Time has an amazing way of showing what really matters.

I cannot explain the effect of Margie's death on my life without including my biggest supporters, God the Father, God the Son, and God the Holy Spirit. Each day I turn to God to give me strength and energy to face life without her. Each day God surrounds my body and soul with love.

It's a joy to look back on the last eighteen months and recognize God's love, faithfulness, and support as I walked the pathway of a spouse's death.

My total happiness will come when the burdens of this earthly life are over and I'm walking through the gates of heaven in the shadow of Jesus Christ.

The events I recorded in my diary focus on:

- o A few life events with Margie
- o A little history of our marriage
- o A lot of godly help
- o A huge amount of grief
- o A record of *The Pain from the Death of a Spouse*

Categories of Death

The death of a loved one is always painful and demanding. I grieved differently for each of my family members who died. My degree of grief relied upon several issues:

Was it a violent death?
Was it a normal death?
Was it a foreseen death?
Was it one of my children?
Was the death an accident?
Was it within my immediate family?
What type of death was it?
How well did I know the person who died?
Did the person die of old age?
How close was our relationship?
Did the person cause his or her own death?
Had the person suffered for a long time?
What was my relationship to the person?

Everyone will have his or her own list of questions to survey when someone dies. I place death in three categories, with each category producing a different type of bereavement.

1. Expected/Forthcoming/Anticipated/Understandable Death
   We all expect to die, if only from old age. Eventually all will die from something. This is the waiting-to-die group. They

have enjoyed life, but they are tired, and the body is broken and weary.

2. Unexpected/Unforeseen/Unpredictable/Shocking Death
This is death prior to old-age death. This death could be from natural disasters or an accidental, by-chance death or sudden death because of health or medical reasons. This is a surprise-death, like a heart attack, stroke, or accident.

3. Complex/Confused/Hard-to-Understand/Can't Believe Death
This is not a simple death. It is a death that is compounded with interrelated activities. It could be a violent death, a death containing emotion or violence or ugliness or intensity, or a death where the person had no control over what happened, like a bomb explosion, a homicide, or a pileup on the interstate, sometimes with multiple deaths. These deaths usually generate the question, "Why did this happen?"

The depth of grieving depends upon the relationship with the person and the way the person died. Grief is personal to each death.

One Remained

Margie Marie (Hall) Rogers (January 17, 1939–May 16, 2012), married July 1956, fifty-five years, ten months. This document will use fifty-five years when referring to married years.

Margie Rogers:	Wife
Buddy Rogers:	Husband
Ed:	Son
Wendy:	Daughter

I am documenting my feelings, my suffering, my distress, my grief, and my thoughts as it relates to the death of my spouse. I plan to record my life events of the next eighteen months. The statements, remarks, and comments will have a relationship and timeline with the past, the present, and the future. The declarations will not be in any type of chronological order. The events will be recorded as they come to mind.

This is my diary of heavenly love, earthly affection, and human pain. It is written with the human side of earth and with the spiritual side of heaven.

When people are sick, we send get-well cards. When people die, we send sympathy cards. I have received both types of cards during my lifetime. Under the current situation, I am the spouse who remains. My friends are sending me cards and encouraging me to get on with life. I want to continue life, and with God's help I will, because God can heal the soul, mend the body, and free the mind. It is easy for God to present these avenues of escape but extremely difficult for humans to do on their own.

If I attempt to heal myself without the help of God, I am headed for a long grieving period and a pain that may never end. I acknowledge the power of God and admit to Him that I cannot do this alone. God will play a huge part in repairing my life. I praise Him for His love and mercy as we work together to free the human soul of *The Pain from the Death of a Spouse.*

Grief is a natural part of the human life cycle. All people will be confronted with grief and pain during their earthly lives. No one is excused or excluded. Yes, even Christians will go through grieving stages when loved ones die. Nowhere in my Bible can I find a statement that says, *"A Christian does not grieve"* or *"It's wrong to grieve."*

God never said I would not suffer pain and grief just because I'm a Christian, but He did say, *"I will never leave you nor forsake you" (Hebrews 13:5 KJV).* I'm holding on to those words with all my strength.

Wow! What a Beginning!

Margie Marie Hall was born on January 17, 1939, to Claude Wesley Hall and Leila (Hough) Hall in Umatilla, Florida. In 1951 Margie and her family moved in next door to the Rogers family. She was twelve years old, and I (Asbury Jr.) was fifteen. To me she was a child, so life went on for a few years without much notice. Margie would come out of her house and turn right to go to school. I would come out of my house and turn left to go to school. She would take a school bus, and I would walk. The Rogers house was in the center of the block, then there was a vacant lot, and then the Hall house. The Rogers house faced south. The Hall house faced west and was on the corner lot. When I looked toward the Hall house, I looked into their back door.

One day I saw a girl walk past our house. She looked to be about sixteen years old, and I asked my family, "Whooooo is that girl?"

They said, "Oh, that's the girl next door."

I said, "Wow."

There was a physical attraction before there was a love attraction. I took a second look, a third look, and a long fourth look. Her attractiveness got my attention. She was beautiful.

My thoughts said, *She is way out of your league, boy.*

I said out loud again, "Wow."

The second, "Wow" was so great that I married her a year and a half later. When my love for Margie started, the love train couldn't be stopped. The love was invisible and irreversible. While I was looking out the front door, love snuck in the back door and got me. Sometimes the heart sees what the eyes can't. In my case, the heart saw love, and the eyes saw beauty.

Marriage Is a Learning Experience

We married in July 1956. Margie was seventeen and a half years old, and I was twenty-one. We were still kids mentally, rationally, maturely, and psychologically when it came to marriage and the responsibility of a family. Our love for each other was about all we had. We did not concern ourselves with all the other things that are needed in a marriage. We didn't have much money. We had a car and a car payment, and we rented a furnished apartment. We were going to see how far love would take us. Well, it didn't take us very far.

It only took one day for us to learn,
> *you cannot live off of love.*

It only took one week for us to learn,
> *two cannot live as cheap as one.*

In the first month of our marriage, we decided to wait a few years before having children. We wanted to get to know each other and make plans for the future. Then we had another marriage learning experience. It only took four months for us to learn,

> *if you don't take precautions, you will be a mama and papa sooner than planned.*

The plan to have children later in our marriage did not reach its goal because twelve months later, we had our first child. We had to mature into adulthood in a hurry as we helped each other grow up and learn the responsibility of caring for a baby and building a family lifestyle.

Another lesson we learned quickly and realistically was

when your	*"outgo"*
is more than your	*"income"*
your	*"upkeep"*
will be your	*"downfall."*

It's a Baby!

Our son was born in the Cocoa-Rockledge Hospital in July 1957. To show how ignorant I was about raising a child, I thought when God created woman, He implanted in her the knowledge and wisdom of how to care for a baby. I thought it was part of a woman's nature. I learned quickly that I had assumed too much. I'd wake up at night, and Margie would be in the rocking chair with the baby. The baby was crying, and Margie was crying. She did not know what to do for the baby. I did learn something from this ordeal: how to make a baby. Our saving grace was Margie's mother. Although she lived in another city, she came to our home to help us for a few weeks. After that, Mrs. Hall was as close as the telephone.

A baby is God's most precious gift. There is nothing in this world more beautiful than a baby in the arms of the mother when they are looking at each other and smiling. You can see a connection between mother and child like no other in the world. Mothers and babies are special.

Years into our marriage, I apologized to Margie for allowing her to take the responsibility of the two children when they were babies. My thoughts that God gave women the insight into a baby's needs is not true. Women do not have a baby-raising instruction manual within them. Margie got her child-raising information from her mother and from anywhere and everywhere. It must have been good information because neither of our children died. Our son was born in July 1957. Our daughter was born two years later, in September 1959.

In March of 1957, we moved to Cocoa, Florida, where we remained for the next fifteen years as I worked at the Cape Canaveral Missile and Spacecraft Proving Ground, locally known as *The Cape*. The Space Center was renamed John F. Kennedy Space Center, in honor of President John F. Kennedy, in November 1963.

I Have a Problem

About ten years into our marriage Margie came to me with a personal problem. She did not know how to explain her issue. She fumbled around, trying to say something without saying anything. I finally said, "Sweetheart, just say it!"

She said, "I'm not as dumb as I look."

She was right. She was beautiful and smart. I was glad she brought her discomfort to my attention. I wasn't trying to keep her out of the decision-making arena; I thought that was the way she wanted it. However, she didn't want it that way. She wanted to have a say and be one of the advisory board members. It did not take me long to realize that her views on family matters and financial affairs made a great contribution in our day-to-day decision making and our long-range plans.

In the early years of our marriage, Margie devoted her life to the duties of a mother and wife. As the kids grew up, she looked toward a career. After several years of schooling and different categories of jobs, she settled at Hughes Aircraft Company in Los Angeles, California. She was the executive assistant on the F18 Fighter Jet Simulator Program. This equipment is the training instrument for the Navy TOPGUN Pilots. Margie worked at Hughes for eighteen years and retired in 1999. We lived in Torrance, California, from 1975 to June 2001. After spending twenty-six years in California, we moved to Valrico, Florida.

Margie loved to travel, and we did as much as we could. Her dream vacation was to go to Australia and New Zealand, so on December 12, 1999, we fulfilled that dream. Margie called it her once-in-a-lifetime vacation.

Serious Sickness

Fast-Forward to 2001

I'll attempt to describe the medical events that led to Margie's death. Her most serious sicknesses began in 2001. For the next five years, she would go from one sickness to another. Sometimes she was attacked by several diseases at the same time. It seemed as if her body was objecting to her going forward with living. Almost every human organ was against her. We knew God was in control and He had a plan to fulfill, so we took our faith and our medicines and waited for God's blueprint to be read and executed.

Without naming her minor ailments, these are a few of the more serious and grave sicknesses that changed our lives dramatically.

Lymphoma Cancer: A group of diseases characterized by progressive enlargement of lymphoid tissue and cells.

Diabetes: Chronic form of diabetes involving an insulin deficiency and characterized by an excess of sugar in the blood and urine.

Bronchitis: Inflammation of the mucous lining of the bronchial tubes.

COPD or Chronic Obstructive Pulmonary Disease: COPD refers to a group of lung diseases that block airflow and make breathing difficult. Damage to the lungs cannot be reversed. It includes cough, fatigue, respiratory infections, wheezing, shortness of breath (that gets worse), trouble catching your breath, chronic bronchitis that involves a long-term cough with mucus, and emphysema, which involves destruction of the lungs.

Asthma: Generally chronic disorder characterized by wheezing, coughing, difficulty in breathing, and a suffocating feeling.

Destroyed immune system: The immune system is a complex network of cells, tissues, and organs that work together to defend against germs.

It helps your body to recognize these foreign invaders. Then its job is to keep them out, or if it can't, to find and destroy them. If your immune system cannot do its job, the results can be serious. Disorders of the immune system cause your immune system to attack your own body cells and tissues by mistake.

Pulmonary, Respiratory, and Pseudomonas

Fast-Forward to 2006

The most serious of these three problems is pseudomonas. Margie acquired the pseudomonas infection in 2006. Pseudomonas infections can develop in many areas of the body, including skin, tissue, bone, ears, eyes, lungs, and heart valves. The site varies with the patient's particular vulnerability.

The most serious infections occur in patients with diminished resistance resulting from other disease or therapy. Pseudomonas infections occur most often by way of cross-infection transmitted from person to person. One person can touch another person and pass pseudomonas along. If I had to describe pseudomonas in a few words, I'd say, "It is a nasty infection, and the results may be deadly."

Our first visit to the infectious disease doctors was in 2006. This visit opened our eyes to how harmful, destructive, and serious pseudomonas infections really are. With medications, the infection can be somewhat controlled for a short period of time. Eventually the medicines will not be able to control the level of the pseudomonas infection, and the angel of death appears.

During the visit, the doctor told us, "If you are having a bad pseudomonas attack and you get pneumonia at the same time, it is a death warrant. There's not a doctor on earth who can save your life. You will suffocate yourself to death. Your lungs cannot provide enough oxygen to the body organs to keep you alive." That statement certainly got our attention.

It felt as if we were dealing with an 800-pound gorilla with a medical problem. This was going to be a tough chore—maybe tougher than we could handle but not tougher than God could handle.

Margie already had breathing problems without adding pseudomonas to the mix. Here is a broad view of how Margie's pseudomonas attacks progressed. I'll use a numbering system to simplify how the disease gets worse and worse. Margie couldn't get back to the health level she was prior to each pseudomonas attack. Pseudomonas, along with pneumonia and the other breathing complications, eventually won.

An example: Margie started with a health level of four, zero being a very healthy person. The pseudomonas attack would drive the infection health level up to thirty. The doctor will give her medication intravenously every day, including Saturday and Sunday, for forty-two straight days. The medicines would drive the pseudomonas infection down to a level of six, but never taking her back to her prior level of four. She was feeling better at level six but not well. Each attack made her weaker and weaker. The next attack might not come for four or five months.

To continue with our example, here comes the next pseudomonas attack. Margie's health level started at six. Again it drove the infection level to thirty. Back to intravenous medicines for the next forty-two days. The medications would drive the infection level down but only to a level of eight. Now she was in jeopardy of getting pneumonia. Margie was getting weaker and weaker and could not fight off the everyday, common diseases. Her life became more fragile. Breathing became more difficult with each attack.

The cycle continued:

> Up to thirty, down to ten
> Up to thirty, down to twelve
> Up to thirty, down to fourteen
> Up to thirty, down to sixteen

Up to thirty, down to eighteen
Up to thirty, down to twenty

The pseudomonas cycles continued year after year, until the medicines could no longer lower the infection level. Eventually she got to the "Up to thirty, down to twenty" level. At this level she had lost 65 percent of her breathing capabilities. Breathing became more difficult and laborious. Her body organs were demanding more oxygen. The demands were greater than her ability to fulfill. Her organs screamed more, more, more, but she didn't have any more.

On November 25, 2011, the day after Thanksgiving, Margie was admitted to the Brandon Hospital. This began her six-month journey to death. I watched her suffer and struggle for months. It hurts to remember this time in her life. It is painful. My vision of her face, arms, and body in the hospitals and rehab are perceptions that I try to eliminate from my memory.

For years we were both healthy and did not know the misery of a serious illness. As we got older and different sicknesses took their toll on our bodies, we were introduced to new diseases.

Heavenly Assurance

Fast-Forward to May 11, 2012

It is a Friday. At about ten in the morning, the rehab center doctor, Dr. Deborah Byrnes, called me aside and said, "Margie will not last a week. I think your children should come for Mother's Day this coming Sunday, May 13, 2012."

I called our son and our daughter, and we made arrangements for them to come to Florida. We used Mother's Day as an excuse for them coming to see her.

Later in the day on May 11, Margie said she was not sure of her salvation.

I said, "Okay, let us forget about the past experience, and we can make it right, right now."

We talked about God and His promises to us. If we believe in Him and ask Him to come into our hearts and save us, He will do it. We prayed, and Margie asked God to come into her heart and save her. A little while later, Margie said she still was not sure-sure. What was giving her disbelief about her salvation was the devil. He wanted to get his last digs in and make her as miserable as possible.

I called our church, First Baptist Brandon, and asked for Rev. David Durham, pastor of the senior adults. Later that day Rev. Durham arrived, and he presented the plan of salvation to Margie, and Margie asked God to save her. She wanted to be double sure that she knew where she was going when she died. I have no problem with that. I was glad she was making sure of her eternity. I love this woman. I am saved, but if I knew for a fact that my spouse died without being saved, I would cry myself to death. It is the worst thing that could happen to a married couple that loves each other. Death of a saved person is one thing, but death without Christ is totally another matter. How can people continue life if they know their spouse is in hell?

Margie wanted assurance that everything was settled and preparations had been made for her arrival in heaven. She had made her reservation in heaven, but she needed assurance that everything was okay. So on May 11, 2012, she and Rev. David Durham spoke to the CEO of Heaven Reservations, Jesus. Jesus personally verified that her arrangements were certain and secure and the reservation was paid in full. She had validated her deliverance from sin and from the penalties of sin. I rejoiced with her when she sealed her salvation to her satisfaction.

Romans 10:9-10 (KJV)

9.   *That if thou shalt confess with thy mouth the Lord Jesus, and shalt believe in thine heart that God hath raised Him from the dead, thou shalt be saved.*

10.   *For with the heart man believeth unto righteousness; and with the mouth confession is made unto salvation.*

Romans 10: 13 (KJV)

13.   *For whosoever shall call upon the name of the Lord shall be saved.*

God Said it,
I Believe it,
That Settles it.

Jesus Christ paid the price for salvation. God created the human race, but we cannot expect Him to overlook sin and call it mercy. God's holiness demands justice. Sin will be punished. There are eternal consequences to everything we do on earth. Death is not the end of the human soul, only the end of the human body. The soul will transfer into eternity.

This life is not all there is. Life on earth is just the rehearsal before the final performance. When we are born, we begin our journey toward eternity. We have to prepare in this life for the next life. Earth is used as the staging area for eternity. Margie's journey to eternity began on January 17, 1939, and ended on May 16, 2012, as she walked into heaven holding hands with Jesus.

I did not learn the true worth and value of her love until she was gone. Now I realize she was priceless. I rejoice in the time we shared for fifty-five years. Time is a gift from God, and it is precious. It's so precious that God only gave it to us minute by minute.

Although Margie traveled the world, there's no comparison to the trip and destination she took May 16, 2012, at 12:30 p.m. God was standing at the gates of heaven, and He welcomed her home. Margie makes heaven even more complete but leaves such a gap in the earthly family. She was kind, loving, caring, warm, and thoughtful. She was a beautiful person, inside and out. She was the sweetheart of my life.

Mother's Day 2012

Sunday, May 13, 2012
Our son and daughter were here to celebrate with their mother. We're happy that Mom was able to enjoy the day with us. We joked, laughed, and teased each other, just like we always do. I write these notes after the fact, and thus I cry as I see Margie in my mind. It breaks my heart to relive the last few days of Margie's life on earth.

Monday, May 14, 2012
Margie is in and out of a coma. Wendy, Ed, and I stayed with her all day. Our son had to return to Washington, DC, for a business meeting that was impossible to postpone, and that was okay. Later that evening Margie was in a state of unconsciousness, and no one was able to bring her back to a wakeful state.

I took our daughter home about six o'clock and came back to the rehab center to be near my sweetheart. I sat in a four-legged chair next to her bed, held her hand, cried, and prayed all night. I would squeeze her hand to let her know that I was there, but she never gave a response. Her hand was cold, but I felt the warmth and emotion of all our yesteryears.

The rehab personnel brought a bed in the room for me, but the bed was too far from Margie. I wanted to be close to her and touch her. Margie was in torment and agony with every breath. She would gasp and struggle for the next one. I thought each breath may be her last. She was extremely weak, and breathing required more energy than she could generate. To watch her in such a battered condition struck at the core of my soul.

The rehab staff was concerned about us, and they came in about ten times during the night to check on us.

I would cry and pray, and then I'd cry and talk to her. These are the four words that I spoke to her constantly during the night: "I love you, Mama."

It was like a song, and there were only four words to sing. I sat close to her in a chair, rocked back and forth, cried, held her hand, and repeated those words several thousand times during the twelve hours that I was with her that Monday night. As I say those words today, it generates a waterfall of tears.

During our fifty-five years, very seldom did I call her *Margie*. Ninety percent of the time I called her *sweetheart*. In shopping centers, in church, at home, in the car, everywhere, it was *sweetheart*. The other 10 percent of the time, I called her *Mama*. When I put the words *I love you* in the statement, it was always a combination of, "I love you, Mama." I said that statement to her thousands and thousands of times during our marriage. I love the woman God gave me.

Tuesday, May 15, 2012

At about seven in the morning I left the rehab center to go home and take a bath. Wendy and I returned to the rehab center and stayed all day with Margie. She was in a coma and did not have anything to eat or drink all day.

I took Wendy home about five in the evening and returned to the rehab center to stay with Margie Tuesday night. At ten o'clock I decided to go home and get some rest. I did not know if I had the toughness to repeat the experiences of last night. I felt guilty about leaving Margie, but maybe a little rest would make me stronger for her.

The Final Good-Bye

Wednesday, May 16, 2012

About 9:30 a.m., Wendy and I walked into Margie's rehab room. She was in a wheelchair and as bright as could be. The thought that came to my mind was what I said to God last night: *Lord, if this is the end, I have not said my final good-bye to Margie.*

God performed a miracle and gave me time with Margie to say good-bye. I took the opportunity to hug her and kiss her and talk to her. I did not say anything to her that might give an indication that this was our final conversation because I thought, *She looks so good. Maybe God is going to keep her on earth a little longer.*

But God had decided to take her home, and He had given me what I asked—a few minutes with Margie. I didn't know it then, but that was our last conversation. God blessed me with the opportunity to tell her once more, "I love you, Mama."

We should take advantage of every opportunity that is given to us to let our loved ones know how much we love them.

The entire rehab staff was shocked at her being awake and by her energy. After we had our time together, the staff said they wanted to give her a bath and clean her room. They did not understand what was happening with Margie because they did not know the power of God.

Wendy and I went to a shady area about ten feet outside the facility for fresh air while they did their tasks. At around ten thirty, the staff called my cell phone and said for us to get back in there!

We rushed back to Margie's room. She was back in a coma. God had fulfilled my prayer request the previous night and had given me extra time with my sweetheart. But just like us humans always do, we want more, more, more. Wendy and I sat next to her bed and held her hands and cried and prayed. There was no movement or sign of life within Margie except for her breathing. Her breathing was such a struggle. I looked at my lifetime partner and cried.

I write the following paragraphs fifteen months after Margie's death. Today is August 16, 2013. I have been working through my grief process and was not in a hurry to revisit the last two hours of her life. These statements describe the suffering and pain Margie was in prior to her death.

As I look backward to May 16, 2012, my heart aches with love pains for my spouse. This was her death day, and it hurt deep inside.

Margie was at a point of no return. The combination of pseudomonas and pneumonia at the same time is too strong to defeat. This was the fourth time for her to have this combination in the last six months. The first three times the doctors battled the sickness and won. They only won the battle because Margie was in a medical facility and the doctors were giving her the strongest medicines the law would allow. The truth is, God was not ready to take her home the other three times. Each pseudomonas-pneumonia attack left her in a weaker state. This time it didn't look good. I hoped Margie could defeat it again, but God had a merciful heart.

The look back produces this vision:

The day was Wednesday May 16 2012.
The place was Brandon Rehab Center in Brandon, Florida.
The time was 10:30 a.m.
Location was rehab room 117.
Margie was in a coma. Wendy and I were sitting next to her bed. We were each holding one of her hands.

Dr. Byrnes was in the room, and she was telling us what to look for as Margie reentered the coma stage: "Margie will take a breath in, hold it for a few seconds, and then she will breathe out. There will be a gap of silence before she takes another breath in. The space of time between when she breathes out and when she takes another breath in will get longer and longer. It will be breathe in, hold a few seconds, breathe out, then silence."

Dr. Byrnes left the room but stayed close. This was the breathing pattern that Margie was performing. The gap of silence between breaths was getting longer and longer. The room door was closed. There were three people present: Margie, Me, and Wendy. It was hard for Margie to breathe. Wendy and I were crying and praying. We were holding her hands. The ever-loving God was present; He was waiting for Margie.

The gaps of silence between breaths were getting longer and longer. It was difficult for her to get the next breath. Each breath was a strain. Her chest was jumping and jerking as she struggled for just a little oxygen. Just a little was all she wanted. Her face was all wrenched as she seized all the oxygen her lungs could suck out of the air. Her lungs were not strong enough to supply the needs of her body. My heart broke as I watched the woman I love in such a painful endeavor. I could not draw a picture of Margie that would represent the stress, the strain, and the effort required to get the next breath. Every second of her life was demanding and painful.

One hour had passed. It was 11:30 a.m. Wendy and I continued to hold her hands cry and pray. There is nothing that we could do but pray. The breathing pattern continued. The silence between breaths increased every minute. Margie was really struggling.

This routine proceeded for another hour. The time was 12:29 p.m. Margie was still in a coma and breathing hard.

Suddenly Margie took a deep breath in. She opened her eyes. She looked into my face and then Wendy's. She quickly looked back and forth. As she breathed out, she said, "I forgive you."

She closed her eyes. We waited for her to take a breath in. It never came. She did not take another breath.

God released her soul to heaven, and then He remained to give comfort and support to the earthly humans who loved her.

I stared at Margie in disbelief. *Is she gone? Maybe she will start breathing again. God help me! What am I to do without her? How will I live without her? How can I function without her?* I became numb, paralyzed, and helpless. *Is this real? Am I dreaming? Is my sweetheart really dead? Am I alive? Oh, God help me.*

Dr. Byrnes came in and pronounced her dead. As I looked at Margie's lifeless body, I did not know what to do. I had never been in this position! Fifty-five years with this woman—I could not live without her! What was I going to do?

In a flash, she was gone. In a flash, she was in heaven. In a flash, she was not suffering. In a flash, I lost a spouse and gained a world of pain.

There are no words that can describe my pain at this moment. I thank God for allowing Margie and me to look at each other one more time before she died.

This is the vision that is embedded in my memory of Margie's last two hours. It still breaks my heart and makes me cry for the one I love. I'm alone as I write these paragraphs, and the words are tearing me apart. The fifteen months between her death and this writing did not erase any of the details, the feelings or the pain I experienced at that moment. I love this woman. Documenting this particular event is more difficult than any of the other things I have written in this diary.

Wednesday, May 16, 2012, 12:30 p.m. became Death Day. This is my D-day. If you live long enough, you will have a D-day of a loved one.

To relive and document the last moments with my darling wife is overwhelming and totally consuming. It is difficult to think of life without her.

How Quickly Circumstances Changed My Life

When a nuclear bomb explodes in a populated area, the human body goes from zero degrees Fahrenheit to ten thousand degrees Fahrenheit in 1.1 seconds. When Dr. Byrnes pronounced Margie dead, I went from hope to devastation in 1.1 seconds. In the same amount of time it takes to destroy the human body with a bomb, my love and marriage were destroyed. The nuclear bomb is instant death. The spouse who remains on earth is dead but not buried, is conscious but not breathing, is hearing but not understanding, is looking but not seeing, is moving but not going anywhere, is alive but not living.

For months after the death of Margie, this was me. Even allowing God to help me, I still felt the human pain, the human suffering, and the human struggle that existed when Margie died. Everything that has happened to me is all a part of this thing we call life.

What words are suitable to describe the loss of a spouse? I don't know if there is a measurement of words that will characterize this type of pain. I cannot tell you how to deal with your grief. I can only tell you of my grief. My first impression of spouse grief was not pleasant because grief delivered intense emotional suffering, physical suffering, mental distress, sorrow, sadness, mourning, pain, anguish, misery, crying, separation, heartache, loss, devastation, anxiety, agony, loneliness, depression, unhappiness, desolation, destruction, and emptiness. Grief knows how to deliver pain.

CHAPTER 2

Money Can't Buy It

The human side of me tried to buy Margie a longer life with medical treatments using artificial, synthetic, chemical, organic, nuclear, and biological medicines. We threw in three hospitals, two rehab centers, different types of medical machines, different types of doctors, and seventy-six days of quarantine confinement. We did all of this within her last six months of life, 176 days of medical care.

Money can buy all of these Things,
                    But Money cannot buy Life.

Money Can't Buy It ....

1. It can buy you Glasses,
                    But not Sight.
2. It can buy you Food,
                    But not Taste.
3. It can buy you Perfume,
                    But not Smell.
4. It can buy you Oxygen,
                    But not Breath.
5. It can buy you a Song,
                    But not a Voice.

6. It can buy you a Piano,
   > But not Talent.
7. It can buy you Cosmetics,
   > But not Beauty.
8. It can buy you a Sound System,
   > But not Hearing.
9. It can buy you Jokes,
   > But not Laughter.
10. It can buy you a Race Car,
    > But not Ability.
11. It can buy you Exercise,
    > But not Energy.
12. It can buy you Vitamins,
    > But not Youth.
13. It can buy you Sky Diving,
    > But not Courage.
14. It can buy you a Resort,
    > But not Relaxation.
15. It can buy you a Parachute,
    > But not Assurance.
16. It can buy you a Gun,
    > But not Bravery.
17. It can buy you Blood,
    > But not Life.
18. It can buy you Medicine,
    > But not Health.
19. It can buy you a Heart,
    > But not a Heartbeat.
20. It can buy you an Operation,
    > But not Healing.
21. It can buy you Insurance,
    > But not Wellness.
22. It can buy you Medical Care,
    > But not Improvement.

23. It can buy you a Rehab Center,
    But not Recovery.
24. It can buy you a Hospital,
    But not Wholeness.
25. It can buy you a Medical Center,
    But not a Tomorrow.
26. It can buy you a Health Club,
    But not Fitness.
27. It can buy you a Playground,
    But not Vitality.
28. It can buy you a Marathon,
    But not Endurance.
29. It can buy you Encyclopedias,
    But not Memory.
30. It can buy you Information,
    But not Wisdom.
31. It can buy you a Book,
    But not Knowledge.
32. It can buy you a Degree,
    But not Understanding.
33. It can buy you a Dictionary,
    But not Comprehension.
34. It can buy you a College,
    But not an Education.
35. It can buy you an Enterprise,
    But not Intelligence.
36. It can buy you a Job,
    But not Experience.
37. It can buy you Companionship,
    But not Friendship.
38. It can buy you Sex,
    But not Love.
39. It can buy you a Promise,
    But not Commitment.

40. It can buy you Pleasure,

     But not Happiness.
41. It can buy you Amusement,

     But not Fulfillment.
42. It can buy you a Spouse,

     But not Truelove.
43. It can buy you a Clock,

     But not Time.
44. It can buy you a Bed,

     But not Sleep.
45. It can buy you a Wedding,

     But not a Marriage.
46. It can buy you a House,

     But not a Home.
47. It can buy you a Valentine,

     But not a Sweetheart.
48. It can buy you a Beach,

     But not a Sunrise.
49. It can buy you a Kingdom,

     But not Joy.
50. It can buy you Authority,

     But not Unity.
51. It can buy you Ego,

     But not Humility.
52. It can buy you Favoritism,

     But not Justice.
53. It can buy you Anxiety,

     But not Patience.
54. It can buy you Acknowledgement,

     But not Honor.
55. It can buy you Applause,

     But not Praise.
56. It can buy you Position,

     But not Respect.

57. It can buy you Servants,
> But not Loyalty.

58. It can buy you Influence,
> But not Acceptance.

59. It can buy you Agreement,
> But not Peace.

60. It can buy you Power,
> But not Obedience.

61. It can buy you Influence,
> But not Acceptance.

62. It can buy you Deception,
> But not Honesty.

63. It can buy you Arrogance,
> But not Modesty.

64. It can buy you Appearance,
> But not Personality.

65. It can buy you Immunity,
> But not Liberty.

66. It can buy you an Endorsement,
> But not Perception.

67. It can buy you a Treaty,
> But not Forgiveness.

68. It can buy you an Election,
> But not Leadership.

69. It can buy you a Pardon,
> But not Freedom.

70. It can buy you a Traitor,
> But not Trust.

71. It can buy you a Roadmap,
> But not Guidance.

72. It can buy you a Security System,
> But not Protection.

73. It can buy you a Warranty,
> But not Reliability.

74. It can buy you Grievers,
      But not Compassion.
75. It can buy you Holy Water,
      But not Holy Spirit.
76. It can buy you Idolatry,
      But not Atonement.
77. It can buy you Doubt,
      But not Faith.
78. It can buy you Baptism,
      But not Belief.
79. It can buy you Theology,
      But not Worship.
80. It can buy you Spirituality,
      But not Conviction.
81. It can buy you a Sermon,
      But not Ministry.
82. It can buy you a Bible,
      But not Salvation.
83. It can buy you a Funeral,
      But not a Soul.
84. It can buy you a Graveyard,
      But not a Spirit.
85. It can buy you a Building,
      But not a Church.
86. It can buy you a Wooden Cross,
      But not a Savior.
87. It can buy you a Rest Home,
      But not a Heavenly Home.
88. It can buy you Christian Facts,
      But not a Personal Bond with Christ.
89. Money, It can buy you Earthly Things,
      But not Heavenly Things.

Money can buy lots of things, but anything you buy, will be left here when you die.

I Timothy 6:7 (KJV)

7.   *For we brought nothing into this world, and it is certain we can carry nothing out.*

Isn't it funny that mankind wants to hold on to this life? Not laughable funny but amazing funny. Why would anyone want to stay here on earth? Heaven is where our Lord lives.

Death, Pain, and Alone

Wednesday, May 30, 2012 (two weeks after D-day)

I had no idea of the pain that would come from the death of a spouse. This is not a pain like you get when you stub your toe and the next day the toe is swollen and hurts. Toe pain can be located and identified. When it comes to Death Pain, it is not comparable with anything in the universe. The Pain is unexplainable and wide spread. The whole body feels the pain but does not know what to do with it. This pain is far beyond my imagination, vision, intelligence and understanding.

The pain from the death of a spouse is:

   a pain of darkness,
   a pain of separation,
   a pain of devastation,
   a pain of consumption,
   a pain of unprepared ness,
   a pain that is actual,
   a pain that is instant,
   a pain that is certain,
   a pain that is specific,
   a pain that is extreme,
   a pain that is decisive,
   a pain that is absolute,
   a pain that is complete,

a pain that is unlimited,
a pain that is immediate,
a pain that is conclusive,
a pain that is within the spirit,
a pain that is within the heart,
a pain that is without description,
a pain that is within the foundation of my soul.

This is my Pain.
> *This is my Life.*
> > *This is my future on earth.*

Rewind to February 2012

About three months into Margie's hospital rehab stay, I asked God, "What am I supposed to learn from this experience with Margie and her sicknesses?" Before He could answer, I said, "The only thing that comes to my small human mind is, 'Learn to live alone.'"

God did not answer because I had guessed what the answer was. Now, I live alone in August of 2012. It is not easy. It is extremely hard to get out of bed each morning knowing it will be a day without Margie. My thoughts of her bring sadness, loneliness, and weeping. These hard times reveal my need of God in ways that good times don't. God doesn't exempt me or anyone from the evidence that we live in a sinful world.

Margie's death is not a tragedy. A tragedy is an airplane crash, a flood, a tornado, a hurricane, avalanche, or anything that is destructive and takes human life or property. God showed His mercy, compassion, and love as He said to Margie, "You have suffered enough. Come home and be with Me."

I'm sure she is praising the Lord right now. My inward spiritual vision of Margie in heaven gives me joy and happiness. But there is another side of mankind—the earthly, sinful side.

The side that wants to cling to the earthly enjoyments of marriage.
The side that wants the other half of the person that we became.
The side that is now a fragile and brittle human.
The side that will remain on earth until God speaks those words to me:
"You have suffered enough. Come home and be with Me."

A Sympathy Note from Myself to Myself

Dear Buddy,

I am so sorry to hear about the death of Margie. I know how much you loved her. She was your best friend, companion, sweetheart, and lifetime partner. Remember that I love and care for you. As you grieve, know that I am thinking of you and honoring the memories of Margie. She will be missed by many. Her life touched me with love and affection. I will miss her smile, her laughter, her character, and her kindness. She will always hold a place in my heart.

I send thoughts of compassion and comfort as you embark on life's journey without Margie. My love, devotion, and support will always be here for you. I will check back with you in a few days to see how I may help you.

Once again, I am so sorry.

With deepest sympathy,

Buddy

Statements of Sympathy

After the death of a loved one, the comments that are made for encouragement may not fit the prevailing condition. I have listed a few statements that family and friends said to me after the death of my spouse. The comments were made in love, but maybe they should have been phrased differently or not said at all. I cannot make recommendations or advise anyone about the pain they are going through. I do not know their personal pain.

I'm sorry to say, I have made ill-advised and improper statements in death situation because I did not know better. I meant well, but I did not know what to say in the face of the most catastrophic event in someone's life. I have learned a lot through my own experiences of family deaths. For one thing, I'm in no position to tell others what they should do or how they should feel because I do not know. Each death has its own character, personality, and pain.

I have included a few of the sympathy statements made to me, and I have noted what I was thinking at the time the statements were being said.

My Opinion of Death Comments

Comments that May Not Be Helpful to the Griever
Think before saying:

1. "You and Margie had a full life together."
   What I'm thinking: "Yes, but I don't want our partnership to end. I have more love to give and to receive."

2. "I know how you feel."
   What I'm thinking: "You can't possibly know how I feel."

3. "Margie is not suffering anymore."
   What I'm thinking: "She's not suffering, but I am."

4. "God will not give you more than you can handle."
   What I'm thinking: "At this moment it feels as if He has given me more than I can handle."

5. "Margie is at peace now."
   What I'm thinking: "I know that, but I'm not at peace in this world of sin and pain."

6. "Margie suffered so much. It is for the best."
   What I'm thinking: "Whose best? Our ring of love and marriage has been broken and cannot be soldered back together."

7. "Margie is in a better place."
   What I'm thinking: "It's comforting to know that, but it doesn't stop my whirlwind of human pain."

8. "If you need anything, call me."
   What I'm thinking: "Do I have to remember to call you in addition to all the other pressing matters?"

9. "The pain will end soon."
   What I'm thinking: "How do you know that? I don't think it will ever end completely."

10. "It may take a while, but in time you will heal."
    What I'm thinking: "That's good to know, but at this moment I do not feel that the world has enough time for me to heal."

11. "In the end, you'll be fine."
    What I'm thinking: "That statement has some truth in it if 'in the end' means when I die because when I die, I will be fine in the Lord."

What I say to myself to shock me back into realization and consciousness is my personal agenda. Everyone will have their own agenda after a family member's death. I may say to myself, "Get over it, Buddy, and move on with life." I have that right. I even have the right to say the above eleven sympathy statements to myself.

Comments and Behavior that May Be Helpful to the Griever
Think, then say and do:

1. "I have no idea of the pain you are in from the death of (dead person's name). Our family loves both of you."
   A little hug may be appropriate.

2. Maybe just a simple comment, like,
   "I'm sorry. Give me a hug,"
   might be sufficient. The human touch does wonders. Whatever is said, it should be earnest and sincere.

3. "I don't know what to say, (griever's name here), but I want you to know I love you and I care for you."

4. In certain cases, there is a silent acknowledgment of the death that is appropriate. Usually close friends and family members do not have to speak because they feel a certain degree of pain. In my case this was true. We saw each other and felt the pain within. We did not speak; we just hugged and cried together.

5. Extend your support and help.
   "I'll stop by in a few days to see if I can help you with (select something that you can do for them):
   washing clothes, washing dishes, cleaning the house,
   grocery shopping, paying the bills, washing the car,
   cutting the grass, things around the house, etc.

6. A hand written note of sympathy is an important expression of love. Let it contain a personal touch of compassion and

condolences in a heartfelt genuine way. Give words of comfort But don't try to cheer the person up with suggestions like the above eleven statements,
'Think, Before Saying.'

My family and friends do not know what is good for me. At this moment, I don't know what is good for me. I'm going to be patient with them and patient with myself.

Remembering

When I talk to God, I talk to Him as Lord and Master of my life. I talk to Him as my Father and me as His child. Sometimes we laugh together. During the writing of this diary, my memories of Margie brought me strong emotional pain.

I would say, "Oh God, these memories bring such pain." Then I would wonder what God could say and what He could do. "Son, if the memories hurt so badly, I can fix that." Then my mind would catch up with my mouth, and I would say to God, "No, Lord, I spoke without thinking. The memories are a gift from you. I don't want them erased. I know You have the power to do that, but I'll put up with the memory pains. Forgive me, Lord."

Then I picture God and me laughing. Be careful what you whine and grumble about to God. He created the universe and all that is in it. He has the power to erase my entire memory with a blink of the eye. I want to hold the precious memories of Margie. One day they will bring tears of joy, but today I pray, "Lord, thank You for the precious memories of Margie. I cry as I think of how much love I have for her. Thank You for blessing me with her love. Thank You for an even greater blessing that will last for eternity—the blessing of life through Jesus Christ, Your Son. Lord, thank You for Your love, grace, mercy, and guidance. Thank You for our talks together, especially the hours You are spending with me during my grief period and for the help I will need in the future. I ask these things in the name of Jesus and for His glory. Amen."

Time Alone

I need time alone, but I also need time with family and friends. I understand the need to talk to someone besides myself and to discuss my pain with others.

The problem I encountered when I isolated myself...... I was the only human I came in contact with, and I only had myself to talk to. If I spend much time with myself, I may start lying to myself about my progress just to feel better. I may even start taking my own advice, and that is scary.

I found a friend who lost his wife a few months after Margie died. We had something in common to talk about, and we gave each other comfort, empathy, friendship, understanding, and encouragement. We both face death emotions, death depression, death pain, death suffering, death fear, death loneliness, death passion, death grief, and death sadness.

We gave ourselves permission to cry, to grieve, to laugh, to be alone, to go shopping, to be with others, to take a vacation, and to do these things anytime and anywhere we felt like it.

I am learning to deal with the reality of my loss. I will grow through this grief experience with love and appreciation.

All Things Work Together for Good

There is a verse in the Bible that I keep repeating to myself:

Romans 8:28 (KJV)
> 28   *And we know that All Things work Together for Good to them that love God, to them who are the called according to His purpose.*

As a Christian, I hold onto to the words of the Lord: "Know that all things work together for good to them that love God."

Not just some things, most things, or a few things.

Not just good things, certain things, or easy things.

Not just close things, helpful things, or choice things.

Not just favorable things, desirable things, or suitable things.

Not just profitable things, honest things, or material things,

But all things. All things work together for good.

I saw this truth when all things were going my way, and I accepted Romans 8:28 at face value. But then my spouse died. Her death affected me immediately, directly, and forcefully. Death is powerful. My world changed instantly.

I asked myself, "How will you survive without Margie?" Then God reminded me of Romans 8:28 and asked me, "What part of the verse is it that you don't understand? All things work together for good to them that love God, to them who are the called according to His purpose."

As I reflect on my life and review the things God has given me and what He promises me, I return to Romans 8:28 with a different viewpoint.

God *did not* promise that my life would always be pleasant, charming, cheerful, and pleasing to me.

God *did not* promise that "all things would work together for good" as I see it as a human being.

God *did not* promise that a single issue would be "good" within itself, as with the death of my spouse.

God *did* promise that, "All things work together for good to them that love Him."

I cannot pick one issue, like my spouse's death and say to God, "I don't see the good in this?"

I can image what God will say: "My child, you may not see the good from your viewpoint because this is My extended view, My design, My truth, My promise, My divine. This is just one thing of the 'all things,' one thing of a larger picture that I command."

Certain single events may be devastating, but each event adds to the "together" objective of God. It takes a combination of single events of life to make the "together" platform that God controls.

"All things work together for good." This "good" may not work together for my enjoyment, my pleasure, my happiness, my comfort, my fortune, or my health but for *good* in God's purpose for all.

The last half of Romans 8:28 reads, "To them who are the called according to His purpose." Not according to my purpose, my will, my plans, my wants, or my mission but those who are called according to God's purpose. When it is within God's purpose, it will be for good that these things have occurred.

CHAPTER 3

Grief Road Maps

There are no road maps, no grief models, no step-by-step guidelines, and no descriptions or instructions for how a person should approach this type of challenge. There is no grading system for where a person should be in three months, in six months, in one year, in two years. There are no charts of grief stages.

I cannot see grief, touch grief, taste grief, smell grief, or hear grief, but I can feel grief right down to my bones. It is impossible to draft a blueprint of grief and pain because:

Each love is different.
Each heart is different.
Each regret is different.
Each person is different.
Each loyalty is different.
Each interest is different.
Each passion is different.
Each emotion is different.
Each marriage is different.
Each sympathy is different.
Each friendship is different.
Each dedication is different.
Each attachment is different.

Each relationship is different.

I do not understand the grief process; it is a mystery. Each day the grief-ghost teaches a grief lesson. I am the student and grief is the teacher. Grief hammers away without pity. Each day I try to move toward recovery and toward a life without Margie. Each day grief teaches the same lesson that was taught yesterday, a lesson of toughness, firmness, and inflexibility. Then grief brags about the environment I have allowed myself to get in, an environment where grief controls.

The daily grief lesson is:

> You have no control over grief.
> You have no idea what grief is.
> You have no restrictions to protect you.
> You have no directions for how to proceed.
> You have no rights when it comes to grief.
> You have no deadlines for relief or completion.
> You have no timetables for when this will be over.
> You have no schedules to tell you what is coming.
> You have no history to inform you of what to expect.
> You have no warnings before being stricken with grief.

I have no say in where grief chooses to go, it has its own agenda. Grief cannot be shared with family or with friends; I must fight this battle alone. I must dress in my flight suit of love and parachute into the wilderness of devastation and misery.

The loss of a loved one is the most dreadful, tragic, and horrifying event that the human will ever experience. There are no medicines or remedies or magical cures for the pain that comes with the death.

When I cut my hand really bad, I'm stressed until I get medical attention and the wound heals. The inner wound that comes from a death is a type of injury that will never completely heal.

Levels, Periods, Degrees, and Stages of Grief

Grief carries with it:

different levels of pain,
different periods of pain,
different degrees of pain, and
different stages of pain.

These are the levels, periods, degrees, and stages of death grief that I went through during the eighteen months I recorded my diary.

A. **May 16, 2012**: I was with my spouse when she died. When she stopped breathing, it was a traumatic, unbelievable, and painful emotional event. I felt my breath being sucked out of me. I became numb. This is the "shock and can't believe" grief period.

B. **May 17, 2012–May 24 2012:** I feel the extreme pain of losing my lifetime partner and love companion. Days and days of crying came with the grief pain. I was still in the shock and can't believe period.

C. **May 25, 2012**: The shock and can't believe period will fade into eternity as it gives way to reality. I know she is gone. We had Margie's funeral on Monday, May 21, 2012. Reality takes over and generates additional degrees of pain, loneliness, and crying.

D. **June 2012–April 2013**: This grief period is a roller coaster of being on the mountaintop and down in the valley. The days repeat themselves with pain, loneliness, and crying. May 2012 started with ups and downs occurring many times a day. At this grief level the downs were very long and the ups were very short.

On the Mountaintop and Down in the Valley

I was exhausted, rundown, and empty. I could not climb another mountain. God says, "I'll climb it with you. Just hold on to Me."

When we got to the mountaintop, I let go of God's hand. I stood there and glared at the wonders and beauty for as far as I could see.

The mountaintop relieved me of so much pressure, and I felt such freedom that I took my eyes off God and stepped away from Him to enjoy what He had given me during my lifetime, especially my spouse. Then all of a sudden, grief grabbed me and threw me on a snowboard, and down the mountainside we went. I had turned my eyes from God and was looking at my fortune of love with Margie. That was my mistake. Grief was waiting for me to be distracted. When I got to the valley of misery, I was flipped onto my back in the meadow of sorrow, regret, and repentance. I was looking at the heavens and staring into the face of God. God was smiling.

I said to God, "Forgive me, Lord. I need Your help to climb this mountain again, and this time I'll stay closer to You."

God said, "Okay. Let's go."

I said, "Thank You, Lord, for being so loving and forgiving."

Each person is unique, and each will have their own personal mountains to climb. Each grief mountain is different in height, in size, in thickness, in strength, in emotion, in stress, and in fearfulness. Climbing the mountain alone is difficult, painful, dirty, polluted, offensive, and tearful.

God is willing to help me over and over and over until I can follow His instructions. His instructions are simple, yet I try to make them complicated and confusing. If I hold onto God, His grip is so strong that nothing can pull me away from Him. As the months passed, the downs became shorter and the ups became longer.

E. **May 2013–October 2013:** I was working hard to put my life back together. It was difficult to accept the loneliness and the single lifestyle. I could see how far I'd come in the last seventeen months, and I considered my current stage as a degree of success. I might be at the degree I must live with until I died. I had come a long way, and God had given me a gift of awareness that told me where I was in my grief experience. I still had a bad day now and then. But overall God had blessed me with love, mercy, and healing. I will never be totally healed from Margie's love, but I will be able to live a meaningful life.

I relate the healing cycles as the growth of a baby. From a baby in arms, to the baby's first steps, to the baby walking unassisted, it takes time and strength to move through the baby stage as with the healing stage. Healing is like the baby walking; it takes time, and it doesn't happen at the same age for every child. Healing will take its own time.

A Pyramid of Daily Grief

Thursday, May 17, 2012 (one day after D-day)

One day after the death of my wife, I cried and prayed all day. I felt such a heavy load of sadness, grief and loneliness. I cried and begged God to help me. I saw Margie in everything I viewed, perceived, and touched. She was such a big part of my life. Our children were present, but they allowed me to have my time alone. God could see my pain, and He would be with me through this journey. The pain felt as if someone had ripped my heart and soul out of my human body. With each breath I was suffocating. Today my crying hours were 80 percent of my waking hours. This was the end of a wonderful marriage. My wildest dreams could not envision the emptiness from a loss of this magnitude. This was going to be the hardest thing I had ever done. The death grief ghost had appeared in my life and wrapped me up in a cloud of darkness. I would dance on the stage of grief and pain for a long time.

The Greater the Love,
The Greater the Pain.

Today I faced darkness, and I cried. I hid myself, and I cried. I thought of Margie, and I cried. I isolated myself in our bedroom, and I cried. I touched her clothes, and I cried. I touched her jewelry, and I cried. I looked at her pictures, and I cried. I felt the quietness of the night, and I cried. I heard the echo of her voice, and I cried. Everywhere I looked I saw Margie, and I cried.

Friday, May 18, 2012 (two days after D-day)

Today was another dark day. I cried and begged God for His mercy. The house seemed larger as I walked through it and thought of the wife who would no longer be. For years I had been told to tell the ones you love that you love them. With my grading system, I never told Margie enough times that I loved her. I told her over and over and over, but it never seemed to be enough times for me. I wanted her to know how much I loved her. To love is to be given a glimpse of heaven, a place where love is supreme and absolute.

During Margie's six-month hospital and rehab stay, we kept setting go-home dates, but the dates never came. She was just too sick. I kept thinking, *If I can get her home, I'll hug her and kiss her and tell her how much love I have for her and be close to her.* I have much love this woman.

Today was more crying, "God, help me." I had a Margie moment, and I cried. I walked through the house, and I cried. I walked outside on our patio, and I cried. I could hear her say, "I need a hug," and I cried. I hugged her stuffed animals, and I cried. I played her music box, and I cried. I looked at her picture, and I cried. I sat in her La-Z-Boy chair, and I cried. I felt the darkness of the night, and I cried. I faced nighttime memories, and I cried.

Then I cried to God, "This is misery. The pain keeps growing throughout my body over and over. I cannot keep myself together physically, mentally, or spiritually. My human body cannot stand the pressure, the tension, the agony, and the burden of losing my spouse. I do not know what I need, Lord. Just help me."

Saturday, May 19, 2012 (three days after D-day)

Today is more of the Thursday's and Friday's proceedings, lots of crying and praying. The human pain is uncontrollable, hysterical, unruly, and unmanageable. It is hard for me to perform a simple task. I'm so lonely for Margie. Oh, I miss her.

Often at nights, Margie and I would lie in bed and talk and touch until the sandman got us, and then we'd drift off into sleepy land. Margie loved to sleep late when she got a chance. I continue getting up early because of the many years that I had to. Even being retired, I still get up at around seven o'clock. When Margie would sleep in, I'd look at her and smile and tell myself how lucky I was. I did not know or understand what would happen if one of us died, yet I knew that one day it would happen. I would quickly put that thought out of my mind.

Sunday, May 20, 2012 (four days after D-day)

I went to church today. It helped to have loving friends around for a little while, but I still need my time alone with God. Nights are extremely lonely. There is stillness in the air. The house is quiet. The quietness almost burst my eardrums. The grieving process consumes my life with sadness, sorrow, and pain. I cry until my face and jaws hurt. Then I cry more because of the pain in my face and jaws from the crying. Fifty-five years of marriage produced a freight train of passion, fondness, enjoyment, and memories. I relived our marriage history, and I cried.

Monday, May 21, 2012 (five days after D-day, day of the funeral)

We had the funeral service at the funeral home in Brandon, Florida. Margie does not have family on the *Hall* side. Her father, mother, and brother died prior to year 2000. I told the Rogers family not to make the trip to Florida. I worry about them out on the road and making such a quick trip back and forth from North Carolina, Virginia, and the Chicago area. Only one of my out-of-state sisters attended the funeral. It is the way I wanted it. No grandchildren attended the funeral. I wanted them to remember Grandma as she was in real life.

My request to our friends in California was not to attend the funeral and not to send flowers. They decided, instead of flowers, they would purchase Gideon Bibles in honor of Margie and Gideon International would be in charge of distribution. That was a wonderful thing to do.

The family that attended the funeral: the husband Buddy, the son Ed, the daughter Wendy. Buddy's sister Peggy Moore and Peggy's daughter and her husband; Tanya and Jon Little. Also Margie's cousin and her husband, Margaret and Scott Reid, from Oviedo, Florida.

Other attendees at the funeral were: Pat and Garney Williams, with over fifty years of friendship; Willie Williams and Jennel Wise from Georgia; and Margie's doctor from the rehab center, Dr. Deborah Byrnes. Local friends, church members, Bible study members, and several leaders from the First Baptist Church of Brandon, Florida, also attended. This is our church where we attend. Dr. Tommy Green, senior pastor of our church, preached the funeral service. David Shenning, music director, sang two songs. Rev. David Durham, senior adults pastor, and Dr. Myles Dowdy, administration director, also attended the service.

Today is Margie's funeral, and I cried. I reflected on our life together, and I cried. I hid myself, and I cried. I remembered our vacations, and I cried. I looked and touched Margie's things, and I cried. I sprayed Margie's Chanel No. 5 Perfume, and I cried. I faced the darkness of a spouse's death, and I cried. *What is life going to be like from now on?* And I cried.

John 11: 25-26 (KJV)

25.   *Jesus said unto her, I am the resurrection, and the life: he that believeth in me, though he were dead, yet shall he live:*

26.   *And whosoever liveth and believeth in me shall never die. Believest thou this?*

And Margie answered, *"Yes"* as God lifted her soul out of the human body and walked her through the heavenly gates.

Could Margie's death be a dream? Am I going to wake up and hug my wife? No, that is not going to happen. This is not a dream. I have lost the woman I love. This is not Disney Land, this is real life. God had mercy on her and took her home. I never prepared for a life without her.

Tuesday, May 22, 2012 (six days after D-day)
Six days after Margie's death and after the funeral, my family returned to their homes. This is a good thing because I need to continue my grief process without interference and interruption. I had cried for days, and the only thing I could say to God was, "God, help me."

That was the only thing I could say. I did not know what to specifically ask God to do for me. God looked into my heart and soul and knew what I needed. My silence of words did not disconnect me from God because He knew my soul. I was lost in a wilderness of pain. I had never felt anything like this. I did not know the depth of pain I would suffer. I needed to be alone with God so we could work on my loss and loneliness. God was helping me face the fact that Margie was gone and she was in a better place. That was my first step in accepting God's mercy and grace.

The Greater the Love,
The Greater the Pain.

Margie is enjoying heaven as I write this diary. If she could see from heaven, she would be unhappy and upset with me because of the mourning, sadness, and loneliness that I was experiencing as a human being. That is why God does not allow Christians to see from heaven to earth or hell. Heaven is a paradise of joy, cheer, and happiness.

I'm holding on to the Word of God.

Matt. 5:4 (KJV)

4.   *'Blessed are those who mourn, for they shall be comforted.'*

Thank God for what you have,
Trust God for what you need.

When God created mankind, He gave us smell, sight, hearing, taste, touch, feelings, soul, warmth, sympathy, passion, love, emotion, and many other attributes and qualities. I found these things and more in my marriage relationship. The things that count in life cannot be counted.

Wednesday, May 23, 2012 (seven days after D-day)
Today is one week since Margie went to be with the Lord. I know the Lord is her caretaker now, and it makes me smile through my tears. This has been a bad week. God and I will get through this together, but it will take adjustments and alterations in my life. It is comforting to know that God is with me. Humans have feelings that must be expressed. I deal with sadness daily, and I envision Margie everywhere in our home. Her beauty and love engulf my heart and soul, and I cry.

Through this experience I have become more sensitive to the pain of others. I now have a view of pain that others suffer by suffering my own through the death of my sister, my father, my mother, my brother, and now my spouse. When the pain is personal, the pain is indescribable and unbearable. I do not understand this kind of pain.

Why Cry?

I started crying as soon as Margie died. I cried almost continually for days. Then I gradually got to a point of only crying maybe five days out of seven, then three out of seven, then only two out of seven. By now months have passed and I'm way down the grief road, but I cry when I want. Even fourteen months after D-day, I'm still emotionally fragile. Out of the blue, some unknown emotion or thing will trigger the cry-fairy. God created humans to have passion and emotions, and I cry whenever it is warranted. I expressed my emotions through tears, through writing a diary of my feelings, through memories of life with my spouse, through talks with friends who knew my spouse, and through prayer. If I had to choose one single event that I did during my grieving that provided me more comfort than any of the other things (not counting God's blessings), I'd have to say, my eighteen-month diary of grief, pain, and suffering. It helped me deliver reality to the death.

Crying is my outward projection of grief and emotion. It should not be considered as degrading or embarrassing or disgusting or outrageous or a shameful act. Crying is the best form of grief release. God supplies every human with this capability, so use it. It does wonders, and then you too can marvel at the results. Crying is a God-given outlet, and there is nothing wrong with crying. Sometimes I lie on my back in our bed and the tears run down my cheeks and into my ears. Over time, the tears will dry upon my cheeks and in my ears, but they will never dry within my heart.

I do not have the words to express my sadness from the death of Margie. My tears give me a release for my pain and substitutes for the unspoken words. It is my pain, it is my grief, and it is my tears. I'm depending upon the love of God to help me through this earthly bitterness.

Emotional Suffering

Grieving has no timetable. Grief did not stand up and suggest an agenda to get over the mourning stages. Grief did not roll out a plan to make life fun again. Grief did not give any information about grieving. Grief only knows one thing: attack.

It takes more than one word to describe the grief from the death of my spouse. The physical and mental anxiety is connected directly to my brain, heart, and nervous system. There is no escape. Grief attacks the innermost avenues of emotions and feelings. What type of pain is it that consumes the life of the spouse who is left behind?

It is love pain and:

It is personal.	It is real.
It is different.	It is internal.
It is unpleasant.	It is intense.
It is stormy.	It is dramatic.
It is explosive.	It is private.
It is physical.	It is overwhelming.
It is hysterical.	It is confusing.
It is frustrating.	It is emotional.
It is unruly.	It is unmanageable.
It is catastrophe.	It is uncivilized.
It is cruel.	It is uncontrollable.
It is expressive.	It is unmerciful.
It is violate.	It is complex.

It is the impact of love.

As I progress through the grief cycle, I encounter pain like ocean waves. The waves of pain come when unexpected, some are large and some are small. At times the large waves roll right over me and consume me with the power of a typhoon. Other times the waves are small and comforting as they splash upon my feet, and then they recede back into the ocean as a sparkling light from God's sunshine.

I must work grief into a position of tiredness so it will have a slower reaction speed. If I can do that, I will be able to escape the grief for short periods of time. First I must loosen grief's grip on me, and I can accomplish that with prayer. Pretty soon I'll be able to sneak away and hide for a few hours with no grief. How do I know that? God said I would.

My Death-Pain Comparison

I'm not sure the English language contains the words that can describe the loneliness, the separation, and the solitude that a person goes through when a loved one dies. In my case, the greater pain came with the death of my spouse than with the death of other family members.

When my sister, Mildred, passed away in 1967 at age nineteen, then my dad, Asbury, in 1969, then my mother, Kathleen, in 1984, then my brother, Jack, age fifty-seven, in 2011, there was pain, but the pain in the death of my spouse is far greater than even the pain of my mother's death. Yes, even greater than the death of the woman who gave me birth. Each experience of loss is unique. My pain experience is different for each of my family members who died. Each is painful in its own right. I do not know the pain of others, as they do not know my pain, because it is my pain. I own it. I love all my family members, but when Margie and I got married, we became one, and over a fifty-five-year period, we became more in love and more as one. At her death, we loved each other more than when we got married.

Margie and I ……. Love and Marriage.

We were two individuals, Yet we became One.

We had two bodies, Yet one Body in Marriage.

We had two hearts, Yet one Heartbeat of Love.

We had two lungs, Yet one Breath of Fresh Air.

We had two brains, Yet one Mind of Togetherness.

We had two noses, Yet one Rose to Smell.

We had two tongues, Yet one Love Song to Sing.

We had two mouths, Yet one Hunger to Satisfy.

We had two heads, Yet one Emotion to Command.

We had two sets of arms, Yet one Hug to Embrace.

We had two sets of feet, Yet one Sandy Beach to Walk.

We had two sets of eyes, Yet one View from the Mountain Top.

We had two sets of ears, Yet one Drumbeat to March By.

We had two sets of legs, Yet one Race to Run.

We had two sets of hands, Yet one Love to Hold.

In marriage we say, "Till death do us part." My love for Margie goes far beyond death. One day, on the other side of human life, I will see Margie, not as a wife but as a child of God. When we see each other, we will know the soul from the past. When Margie died she was with the Lord in a flash. She does not remember any of the earthly activities or the people who remain on earth.

Rev. 21:4 (KJV)

4.   *'And God shall wipe away all tears from their eyes; and there shall be no more death, neither sorrow, nor crying, neither shall there be any more pain; for all former things are passed away.'*

The last seven words of that verse clearly tell me, "For all former things are passed away." I believe all earthly things are removed from the memory of a saved person as soon as he or she dies. I also believe that when I get to heaven, I will be able to recognize Margie's soul and she will recognize mine. Today I don't believe Margie knows that I exist.

I Corinthians 13:12 (KJV)

12.   *For now we see through a glass, darkly; but then face to face: now I know in part; but then shall I know even as also I am known.*

Initial Shock about My Spouse's Death

Rewind to May 16 2012 (D-day)

On May16, 2012, at 12:30 p.m., Margie died. As I departed the rehab center, I stepped out into a universe I had never seen before. I walked out the door and into a forest. A forest of trees began to grow around me with each step. They grew taller, thicker, and darker as I stepped deeper into them. They began to surround me, touch me, and squeeze me. The trees were choking the life out of me. I couldn't breathe. I have never been in this type of environment. It was very dark. I could not locate my car; the trees had blocked my view. I couldn't get my breath. I was being smothered. I couldn't see for the darkness. The trees were choking me. They were crowding me with more and more force. What was happening?

I stopped walking and the trees stopped growing. We were at a standstill and a stand-off. If I didn't go forward, the trees didn't grow thicker, taller, and darker. I could not see.

I cried out to God, "Help me, Lord. I cannot see. This is the darkest time of my life. I have lost my earthly love and my earthly way."

God knew this situation would happen to me before I was ever born, but like every father, He wanted me to ask Him for His help. I wanted God's help; I needed God's help.

All of a sudden I heard a buzz saw, and the trees began to fall, but I saw no one. The darkness was being replaced with light. The trees were being cut down, and they were falling away from me. They continued to fall, yet I saw no saw and no man. Shortly I saw no standing trees; they were all on the ground next to their stumps. Then the trees and their stumps were sucked into the earth and the ground became hard and smooth.

I saw my car. I walked to it. I sat down in it. Every element of my body cried out to God for His help. I did not know what I was going to do without Margie. The loss struck at the foundation of my human mind and soul.

Nothing could have prepared me for the death of my spouse. The death of my family members did not prepare me for what came on May 16, 2012. The agonizing emotional pain is devastating. I wanted to run and hide, but that wouldn't change anything. I had to face the facts; my spouse was physically gone. Facing the facts did not happen immediately. I was so overwhelmed that it took a week to recognize the facts and longer to accept the facts.

A Life of "No Mores"

This was the beginning of a life without my sweetheart. The commodities of marriage would no more be. They will become the articles of a *no-more* environment, and they are the *trees* that were around me and were pulled into the earth.

The silent scream of grief and pain are far beyond my vision and understanding. If I wish to continue life, I must adapt a *no-more* attitude, disposition, and mental state in the Margie-and-I relationship. I must adjust to the things that I will crave and long for in our relationship characteristics.

No more ... No more ... No more ...

No more hugs,
No more kisses,
No more attachment,
No more humor,
No more bonding,
No more affection,
No more emotion,
No more calmness,
No more embracement,
No more passion,
No more fondness,
No more "Just a minute,"
No more loyalty,
No more "I love you,"
No more holding hands,
No more desire,
No more sharing,
No more appreciation,
No more walks,
No more discussions,
No more conversations,
No more concern,
No more playfulness,
No more understanding,
No more flirting,
No more connection,
No more chat times,

No more caressing,
No more "Be careful,"
No more commitment,
No more romance,
No more making up,
No more debates,
No more love,
No more sincerity,
No more dependability,
No more winks,
No more attraction,
No more endearment,
No more caring,
No more date-nights,
No more companionship,
No more regard,
No more courtship,
No more contentment,
No more consoling,
No more soothing,
No more infatuation,
No more enjoyment,
No more closeness,
No more indulgence,
No more devotion,
No more gentleness,
No more sentimentalism,

No more adoration,

No more "Drive safely,"

No more phone calls,

No more presence,

No more love cards,

No more caring for,

No more honoring,

No more laughter,

No more cherishment,

No more respect,

No more touching,

No more laughing together,

No more giving her red roses,

No more singing together,

No more vacations together,

No more crying together,

No more teasing,

No more admiration,

No more special moments,

No more kindness,

No more friendship,

No more "How do I look?"

No more tenderness,

No more eye-gazing,

No more, "You love me?"

No more praying together,

No more worshipping together,

No more quietness,

No more truelove,

No more smiles,

No more support,

No more warmth,

No more looking out for each other,

No more, "Let's go to breakfast,"

No more togetherness,

No more smell of Chanel #5.

No more … No more … No more … ninety no mores

I cried as I composed these *no-more* words.

Saturday, March 16, 2013 (ten months after D-day)

It has been ten months since Margie's death, and I still cry as I *reread* the *no-more* phrases above. These are the things that held us together. I keep telling myself that I'm healing and progressing toward a life without Margie. But then a thought or a sound or a glance at her picture and my mind brings back her death memories and her living memories. I'm trying to dwell on the good things in our marriage, but the good things remind me of what I will not have anymore.

The *no mores* do not stop here. There is the other side of marriage. Yes, we had two sides. These are the things that are in every marriage. Margie and I were two different people. We complemented each other with our differences. But sometimes the differences got in the way. We didn't like to find the areas where we did not see eye-to-eye because they generated their own list of *no mores* and made us uncomfortable with each other.

These *no mores* only existed at the time of disagreement and for a short period thereafter. But as I look back at those times and issues, they were so insufficient I cannot remember even one of them. The *no mores* below will not be missed.

I believe that during any marriage these issues will present themselves.

No more … No more … No more …
No more tension,   No more clashing,   No more disagreements,
No more disputes, No more criticizing,   No more irritabilities,
No more anxiety,   No more spats,   No more bickering,
No more blaming,   No more complaining, No more controversy,
No more anger,   No more altercations,   No more objections,
No more issues,   No more stress,   No more being defensive,
No more discord,   No more misunderstandings.
No more speaking sharply   No more … No more … No more …

When Margie and I were in agreement and harmony with each other, the above *no mores* did not deserve a second thought, and they could not be found anywhere in our home. However, they were always near.

We had different personalities so we had discussions and disagreements, but when all was said and done, we still loved each other. The ill feelings usually lasted a day or so. But even through those times, we would have fought till the death for each other.

At bedtime Margie would say to me, "I don't want us to go to sleep being mad with each other." But sometimes I did. I wanted to stay mad. I wanted her to know that I was upset with her. I would not say, "I'm sorry" before she went to sleep. After she went to sleep, I would take my hand and move it toward her until I touched her body, and knowing she was lying beside me gave me great comfort.

I would softly whisper, "I'm sorry. Forgive me. I love you," usually too soft for her to hear me.

That was the devilish side of me. A new day usually started with both of us wanting to forget yesterday. I cannot think of one subject that caused an argument, a discussion, or a disagreement because the total sums of them *all* amounts to zero, zero, zero.

As I read these statements today (year 2013), I'm so glad Margie did not die during the night. She wanted to discuss our differences before going to sleep, but I didn't. If she had died, I would not have the opportunity to say, "I'm sorry. Forgive me. I love you." That guilt would have hung around my neck until I died. Now I realize that Margie was right; we should not go to sleep mad at each other. I'm glad I did not learn that lesson the hard way.

When a person dies, God invokes His own *no-more* declarations for the saved person and for the lost person.

For the saved person, there will be:

No more death,	No more tears,
No more sadness,	No more pain,
No more sorrow,	No more loneliness,
No more grief,	No more sickness,
No more suffering,	No more separation,
No more darkness,	No more unhappiness,
No more solitude,	No more isolation,
No more harm,	No more mourning,
No more gloom,	No more depression,
No more disease,	No more difficulty,
No more hardship,	No more unrest,
No more sin,	No more wickedness.

For the lost person, there will be:

No more opportunities to be saved.

Ten Things a Lost Person Will Discover, One Second after Death.

1. One second after death the lost person will discover that –
    Death did not end it all.

2. One second after death the lost person will discover that –
    Satin has lied to them.

3. One second after death the lost person will discover that –
    Hell is real.

4. One second after death the lost person will discover that –
    Everyone will live eternally, in Heaven or in Hell.

5. One second after death the lost person will discover that –
    God has a record of all their sins and He can see the sins of a lost person.

6. One second after death the lost person will discover that –
    They still have memories of their life.

7. One second after death the lost person will discover that –
    They are consumed by the works of their own hands.

8. One second after death the lost person will discover that –
    They missed the most important thing in life, knowing God.

9. One second after death the lost person will discover that –
    The opportunities they had to be saved are gone, and gone forever.

10. One second after death the lost person will discover that –
Life's Short,
    Hell's Hot,
        Eternity's Long.

Tuesday, May 9, 2012
Seven days before Margie died
The rehab center doctor, Dr. Deborah Byrnes, was examining Margie, and she asked Margie what her favorite candy bar was. Margie said she liked Snickers but could not eat the peanuts in her current condition. Her second choice was a Milky Way.

At about two o'clock in the afternoon, Dr. Byrnes returned to Margie's room, and she had the largest Mickey Way bar I have ever seen. She had gone out during lunch and purchased the candy for Margie. Dr. Byrnes cut the candy bar in half and said, "Eat half now, and we'll eat the other half later." Margie ate as much as she could and said, "That was really good."

Margie never ate the other half of the Milky Way. She died a week later. Dr. Byrnes came to Margie's funeral. She signed the registration book, and this is what she wrote" "I won't be able to eat a Milky Way bar without thinking of her" (Margie).

Fast-Forward to August 31, 2012 (three months after D-day)
The grief ghost has been very active since May 16, 2012. I can't seem to get away from it. I try to make grief mad enough to leave, but it doesn't. It may disappear for a short period, but when it comes back, it comes back with vengeance and with an appetite for pain. If I get away for a few hours, grief goes insane and attacks me at first sight. Deceitful little booger, it has no character. Grief never takes a day off, never sleeps, and never eats. I can't see it or touch it, but I can feel it. It has been a constant ghost in my life since May 2012.

Sometimes I tell myself that I'm doing pretty-good with the death pain. Then I realize that I do not know where the grief ghost is. I tiptoe around the house because I want to get to sleep before grief finds me. All of a sudden grief springs from its hiding place, tackles me, and then body-slams me to the floor with memories of Margie. Grief is taking control again tonight.

I'd like to leave grief at home, but it's almost impossible. I cannot get in the car and back out of my driveway fast enough to leave grief. I'm currently taking baby steps, but I'm making distance down the highway of recovery.

Getting Things Done Four Months after D-day

September 20, 2012

I'm trying to get something done around the house today. I'm not planning a lot of activities. My mind is confused, and it is not doing things in any type of order. I did not rest good last night. I dreamed about Margie. I have one objective today: washing the outside windows.

I back the car out of the garage and park it next to the curb. Here comes Fed-Ex with a package. It is from a friend in California. I look in the box to see what they sent. It's See's Candy—goooood candy. I put the candy in the trunk of the car because I might eat a few pieces while washing the windows.

I really want to be constructive today. I haven't done home projects since Margie died. The outside of the house has not been cleaned in six months; it doesn't carry a high priority. Recently, the grief process has taken most of my time.

Sure is hot today. Thunderstorm weather; must be ninety degrees. As I pull the hose from the south side of the house, I notice the hose is too short. I'll need the other hose. As I go to get the longer hose, I notice that the squirrels have eaten my potted plant that I had at the funeral.

I say to myself, "I'm going to get those little boogers!"

I had hoped to keep the plant for several years. Three weeks ago I purchased flower seeds that I was going to plant around that pot. I left several packages of seeds next to the pots. I'll plant the seeds somewhere else after I wash the windows.

I go to get my nozzle-mop to hook to the longer water hose to clean the windows. Oh, here comes the mail. I have a lot of mail today. I look at it for about fifteen minutes. Some of it will need attention tonight. I'll put the mail in the car trunk with the candy. I'm not going to take the mail in the house right now because my shoes are dirty and mopping the floor is not on the schedule. As I place the mail in the trunk of the car, I observe about ten Sunday newspapers in the trunk that my neighbor gave me to recycle. I took the newspapers out of the trunk and placed them on the lawn. I'll get the recycle containers from the backyard later and put all the papers in it and place the containers at the curb before dark.

Since garbage collection is tomorrow, I think I'll clean the trash out of the car when I get the trash cans around front. I don't want to lose the keys while working around the house so I'll toss them in the floorboard of the car.

Oh, here comes one of my neighbors. He needs someone to hold his ladder so he can get on his house to remove several limbs and the leaves that have collected on the roof. This may not take long. Okay, we're finished. It took longer than I thought. I'll get back to my work.

I should rake the leaves before I wash the windows because they will be easier to rake if they are dry. I'll pick up the limbs in the yard before I rake. I'll start in the backyard. Since I'll be in the backyard I should lock the car because my portable GPS is in there. Better close the garage door too.

I'm ready to pick up the limbs in the backyard. I'll use two cans for the limbs and two cans for the leaves. I have lots of limbs on the ground. I'll need two large trash bags to place in the two garbage cans to hold the leaves.

Wait a minute! Do I feel raindrops? It's getting darker as the clouds cover the sun. It's beginning to rain. I'm not ready for rain!

This is not the day that I planned. It is raining. So here I am, standing in the front yard and staring at the heavens as it rains in my face:

o the garage door is down
o the car still has its trash
o the tree limbs are still on the ground
o the leaves are still covering the grass
o the two water hoses are on the front lawn
o the candy is melting in the trunk of the car
o the newspapers have blown down the street
o the recycle containers are still in the backyard
o the mail in the trunk needs to be reviewed tonight
o the two garbage cans for the leaves are still in the rack
o the keys to the house and the car are locked in the car
o the potted plant we had at the funeral is nothing but dirt
o the squirrels tore the flower seed bags open and ate the seeds

I stand here in the rain, soaked to the bone and I wonder, *What did I accomplish today?*

I thought a little activity would give me a break from the grief, but now I'm grieved and stressed. It's another day in the life of the spouse who is left behind. The human remains of a grieved person.

I Married the Girl Next Door

A few years into our marriage I started teasing Margie about us getting married. These are the words that I repeated to her many times.

I'd say, "You know, back in the 1950s, it was love for country, Mom, apple pie, and the girl next door. Even the movies were directed that way. There was always a movie-love situation for the girl next door. They would get married and leave the impression of happiness forever. Now I discover that the movies are not real life. It's fiction. They didn't really get married! I've been tricked! I didn't know I had a choice. I thought I had to marry the girl next door! I didn't know I could choose someone else! I've been outwitted and abused! I was caught off guard! I was taken advantage of! I've been mistreated! It's not fair. This is a lifetime sentence!"

This is what I said to her many times during our marriage. Then we'd laugh, and hug each other. I married the girl next door because I loved her. I am the winner because I got a sweetheart and a spouse.

Today is November 16, 2013, eighteen months after D-day. I cry as I read the above, "I married the girl next door."

What a blessing God gave me. I still love that woman.

CHAPTER 4

One Year after D-Day

May 16, 2013

One year after the death of Margie (D-day, May 16, 2012), I cry as I rewind and relive the two hours before she died. It has been a year, but the events are as fresh as yesterday. Death did not end the love I have for her. I thank God for His mercy because He loved her enough to stop her suffering and to take her to His home.

Margie was in the hospital and rehab for almost six months. Each day I watched her suffocate, little by little, until she no longer had the strength or endurance to survive the enemies of sickness. I saw her getting weaker and weaker, but I could not shield her or protect her from the afflictions. Fifty five years of marriage, looking out for her and loving her, did not give me the authority or the right to ask God to prolong her suffering on earth for my benefit.

God allows things to happen in our lives to teach us things He wants used for His glory. Currently I do not see or understand what God wants me to do with the information I gathered through my experience of a spouse's death. I pray that God will help me find a way to put my sorrow to good use. I want to find a way to turn the grieving and mourning into some type of positive expression. God loves His children, and He will give me the strength and love I need to get through this experience.

Taking Spouses for Granted

There comes a time in marriages when we often take our spouse for granted. I did not know how much I loved Margie until she died. If I had known the true love I had for this woman, it may have been destructive to our marriage. I think I would have smothered her to death by holding her, kissing her, and touching her all the time. She would have told me, "Get away from me. You're driving me crazy." Her death may have been death by love suffocation.

Margie told me countless times, "I love you with all my heart." I did not know the true depth of that type of love until Margie died. Now I know what she meant. Margie knew the true value of love, and she understood the love Paul spoke of in the Bible in 1 Corinthians.

I Corinthians 13:2-3 (KJV)

2b.   and though I have all faith, so that I could remove mountains, and have not charity (love), I am nothing.

3.   And though I bestow all my goods to feed the poor, and though I give my body to be burned, and have not charity (love), it profiteth me nothing.

As the saying goes:

'You can give without loving,

but you cannot love without giving.'

Writing My Diary

June 16, 2012 (one month after D-day)

Today is one month into the grieving process. It is difficult to write about my feelings today. I cry as I write. I'm beginning to wonder if it is a good idea to create a diary. I don't know if it is helping me or prolonging the grief process. Who do you ask? I don't want advice from a person who has not been through the death-of-a-spouse grief process. Therefore, not knowing the results one way or the other, I'll do what I want, and I want to record how I feel and what I feel. I'll continue writing in my diary.

References to Death

It's amazing how we refer to death and the wording we use when someone dies.

Die: Is the basic, simple, direct word meaning to stop living.
Decease: This is the legal term.
Expire: This means literally to breathe one's last breath.
Pass Away: Suggesting a coming to an end.
Perish: Implies death by a violent means or under difficult circumstances.

But then we use words for death such as:

o   croacked
o   was taken
o   keeled over
o   faded away
o   bit the dust
o   checked out
o   fell asleep
o   resting in peace
o   gone to glory
o   gone belly up
o   bit the bullet
o   suffered death
o   dropped dead

o   bought the farm
o   returned to dust
o   relinquished life
o   closed one's eyes
o   kicked the bucket
o   gave up the ghost
o   pushing up daisies
o   laid down one's life
o   cashed in one's chips
o   gone to one's rewards
o   took one's last breathe
o   gone to one's last home
o   joined the great majority
o   gone to the great beyond
o   paid the supreme sacrifice
o   breathed one's last breath

But regardless of how we refer to death, it is something we will all take part in. Margie was extremely sick the last few years of her life, and she was unable to sleep in a bed. She could not breathe lying down. She could breathe better sleeping in a La-Z-Boy chair. I did not want to be very far from her, so I slept on a couch near her for about two years. I didn't mind; I wanted to be close to her.

As her outward beauty faded, her inward beauty grew, and my love for her grew more each day. After she passed away, I continued to sleep on the couch for nine months before I returned to the bedroom. I felt depressed and disoriented. God's thought within me keeps leading me toward recovery, but total recovery will not come until I'm with the Lord. Margie will always have a place in my heart.

You Know What I Think I'll Do?

About 1980, Margie and I established Friday night as our night. This night was just for us. Our kids were out of the house and own their own. It was pizza, salad, and a movie at home. Our time. One night we had finished eating and were relaxing getting ready to watch our movie.

I said, "You know what I think I'll do?"

She said, "What?"

I said, "I think I'll go to the grocery store and get some ice cream." I kept sitting there. Fifteen minutes later, I said, "You know what I think I'll do"

She said, "What?"

I said, "I think I'll go to the grocery store and get some ice cream," and again, I kept sitting there.

Ten minutes went by. Margie said, "Are you going to get the ice cream?"

I said, "Iiiiiii don't think so."

She said, "I want some ice cream!"

I said, "Okay, I'll go get some." And I did.

Months later I found another issue to insert into the, "You know what I think I'll do?" game. I enjoyed playing this with Margie, and it was something personal to us. We'd be sitting around, in a relaxing mode and enjoying our time together.

I'd say, "You know what I think I'll do?"

She's say, "What?"

I'd say, "I think I'll strip off naked and run through the house."

She'd say, "If that's what you want to do!"

I'd keep sitting there. Ten minutes later, I'd say, "You know what I think I'll do?"

She'd say, "What?"

I'd say, "I think I'll strip off naked and run through the house."

She'd say, "If that's what you want to do!"

I'd keep sitting there, and ten minutes would go by. I'd say, "You know what I think I'll do?"

She'd say, "What?"

I'd say, "I think I'll strip off naked and run through the house."

She'd say, "All that is going to get you, is you'll be *hot, tired,* and *sweaty.*"

We'd laugh and hug each other. This established a routine that I did six to eight times a month for the rest of her life. I loved to play this game with her.

I loved it when she said, "All that is going to get you, is you'll be hot, tired, and sweaty."

I can still hear the echoes of those words, but now, there are no laughs and no hugs.

The message I received from the words themselves and Margie's tone of voice was, "If you think that act is going to get me excited, you're badly mistaken, confused, and misinformed."

I smile as I think of the many times we repeated this process. We played this over and over for years. I'd say the same words, and she'd say the same words. I never stripped naked, and I never ran through the house.

We had other amusements that we enjoyed, but this was my favorite. These are types of things that enriched our marriage and made it worthwhile. They were all ridiculous, silly, and stupid, but we both enjoyed the laugh and irrational behavior. I've always been a little crazy, but it took Margie several years to grow into an insane conscious. Two people who enjoy laughing, joking, and teasing can develop a distraction that builds a close relationship of love.

A Cedar Chest

Shortly after we got married, Margie asked me to buy her a cedar chest. It was to be her personal property, and I was to never look in it. It was her business. I bought her the chest two months after we got married. I promised to never look in it, and for fifty-five years I never did.

The Wedding Dress

August 1, 2012 (eleven weeks after D-day)

This is the first time I have opened Margie's Cedar Chest since I gave it to her in October 1956. This was her personal property, and I promised her that I would never look in it. I was surprised at what I found. The chest contained a few new clothing items that she had purchased and hid away for later. They still had the price tags on them. It was her business. I'm glad she played this hide-and-seek game with me because it gave her pleasure. I smile as I think of her and the games she played to put something over on me.

The biggest surprise I found in the chest was Margie's wedding dress. She never told me the dress was in the chest. I thought we had lost the dress years ago so I would never ask about it. The last time I saw the dress, it was on Margie at the wedding. Margie left the dress with her mother on our wedding night.

Mrs. Hall came to live with us a few years before she died. She must have brought the wedding dress at that time, but I didn't see it. Nevertheless, I never asked Margie about the dress because it would only bring sad feelings if it was lost.

I took the items out of the chest and looked at them. I cried for about an hour as I envisioned her in the wedding dress in 1956. Later I placed all the articles back in the chest.

Margie's Personal Things

July 13, 2012

I am tired, weary, and burned out. I have been on this crying merry-go-round for weeks. Margie is everywhere. I touch her picture, and I cry. I touch her shoes, and I cry. I touch her make-up, and I cry. I touch her pillow, and I cry. I touch her purses, and I cry. I touch her blouses, and I cry. I touch her pantsuits, and I cry. I touch her dresses, and I cry. I touch her nightgowns, and I cry.

There is not a place in this house that does not remind me of Margie. I can go to any room and I see Margie. I can go to any closet and I see Margie. I can go to any bathroom and I see Margie. She is all over this house, and I see her dressed in all of her personal things. Seeing Margie's earthly possessions every day is eating me up. I cannot allow these worldly goods to control my grief. These things are just things, just items of necessity.

Why am I punishing myself? There are so many people who can use Margie's personal belongs. I'm going to give her personal things away, and I do not feel any guilt in doing so. This gesture of goodwill does not disrespect or disgrace or dishonor or discredit my love and admiration for Margie. If Margie could speak from heaven, she would say to me, "Don't look at my belongs and let them affect you. Our marriage and love were more than possessions. Don't degrade what we had; we had more than that. Give my stuff to the needy. It's only stuff."

I will honor Margie's earthly existence by giving family members certain items that will keep her memory alive in the minds of the current generation and grandkids beyond. Ninety-eight percent of her stuff will be given away.

September 22, 2012
Four months after D-day, I have completely removed Margie's clothing items and shoes from our home. About 90 percent went to our church, First Baptist Church Brandon, and 8 percent went to ECHO. Our church stocks clothing, shoes, and groceries and gives these things away to the needy. I'm glad God blessed us with possessions that allowed us the opportunity to bless others. The only clothes I kept were Margie's wedding dress and a red dress that I loved to see her wear.

I don't need to see her personal items every day. I don't need to envision her in the illusions. I don't need to add more sadness and sorrow to my already depressed state.

Neutral Ground in a Marriage

Rewind to 1969
In 1969 Margie and I were participating in a revival at our church. One night the visiting preacher's message was about marriage relationships. He said all couples have disagreements and there should be a neutral area—a place where you can go clear up the matter at hand. A place where you can talk it out, a time-out area. It could be the dining room or the garage or a bathroom. Of course, being a man (now, don't get ahead of me), I wanted the area to be our bedroom. So Margie said okay, but she knew it would not work. Going to the bedroom upset never worked for us. Maybe if we had picked the living room or the bathroom it may have worked, but the bedroom—no way. It did not work. How can you be upset one minute and loveable the next?

Margie was good about letting me have my way to prove a point. After a few visits to the bedroom's neutral zone where nothing was accomplished, Margie told me, "You think the bedroom is the solution for everything. If I don't stop coming in the bedroom with a bad attitude, I may have a bad attitude every time I come in here."

I said, "Maybe we should have our neutral area under the shade tree in the backyard."

She really knew how to let me down easy without me even knowing it. I look back now and smile at some of the things she did and the enjoyment she got out of it. I love her for it.

The Move from Florida to California

Fast-Forward to 1974.

In 1974 we lived in Brandon, Florida, and I wanted to make a move in my employment position.

I presented a major problem in our marriage when I flew from Tampa to California and interviewed with Continental Airlines for a position that I thought would be best for my career. It was a challenging and demanding task that would stretch my knowledge of computers and system designs to the limit. Continental was still in the second-generation DOS environment while the rest of the world was on the computer OS fourth-generation stage.

I interviewed with two upper management personnel, and they wanted me to interview with the vice president of Continental Airlines. While interviewing with the VP, we were interrupted by a problem that they had been working on for several days. Continental was trying to find some particular computer records. I suggested a solution to their current problem and how to fix their system for future lookups. Instead of taking days, it would only take seconds to locate any record. Once we established the new types of databases that were available to us, we'd be prepared for all future record-finding requests. The VP offered me the job, and I took it.

I took the position without discussing it with Margie or the family. I was not fair minded to demand such a move. Margie was born and raised in Florida. As far as she was concerned, California was a foreign country. I was selfish and self-centered, with no concern for my family's feelings. In my own defense … as head of the household, I felt the responsibility of a family and me providing for them. I was looking to the future and where I wanted to be five to ten years down the road. I wanted the best for them but went about it the wrong way.

This is a time in our marriage when there were no plans to move to another city, let alone to another state. The "let alone" words turned out to be true because I ended up in California alone.

And Margie was saying, "Leave me alone because I'm mad."

This is one of those times where the disagreement lasted more than one or two days. I moved to Los Angeles after Christmas 1974 and started to work for Continental Airlines first week of January 1975. I said I because the rest of the family was unsure of their desires and destination. I love my family and I wanted them with me, but I caused the problem. There is always something to be learned when a decision is made by one spouse and not both of them together.

And what did I learn? *I'll never do that again.*

I wrote Margie a letter every day. When I say every day, I mean seven days a week. Every day for nine months I tried to explain my position. The family was in Florida, and I was in California. No one was happy. It took a while before we started making family plans for our future.

The Continental vice president understood my problem and told me, "Anytime you want to go to Tampa for a few days, just do it."

And I did, nine times between January and September. We moved on my tenth trip back to Florida.

While going through Margie's personal items today (August 16, 2012), I came upon some of the letters that I wrote to her when I was living in Los Angeles and the family was in Florida. This is the first time I have seen these letters since I mailed them to her in 1975. That is thirty-seven years ago as of 2012. I did not know she saved the letters. I told her to destroy them. I did not want the kids to see the letters and determine that she and I were having a problem. We were having a problem, but I did not want the kids to worry about it

Loneliness

With the family being apart for months, I got a taste of loneliness and I did not like the flavor. However, this type of loneliness does not ripple the water compared to the typhoon loneliness waters of a spouse's death. The California loneliness was not permanent, just a temporary loneliness situation. I knew where she was, and I could get to her and the family within eight or nine hours.

In September 1975 the family moved to California. The drive from Brandon, Florida, to Torrance, California, took five days, twenty-eight hundred miles. My son, Ed, and I drove across country. Margie and our daughter, Wendy, flew. Margie had told me earlier in our marriage that she wasn't as dumb as she looked. She proved that point once again and received another point on her side of the ledger. Our son and I seemed to be the ones who were outsmarted because we were the ones who drove across America.

Death Loneliness

Death loneliness is devastating. The dictionary describes loneliness as lonesomeness, solitude, detachment, separation, desolation, aloneness, isolation, unhappiness, and longing for. Loneliness carries an emptiness that grips a heart and soul and then vacuums the life out of that person.

The person becomes a shadow and a mirrored reflection of their original frames.

Loneliness pitched a hundred-mile-an-hour fastball and smashed my heart like a window pane. So far in my life, there is no pain that can compare to the consuming pain of the death of my spouse.

Loneliness is like a thermometer in the desert that goes to its highest point during the day and at night drops to its lowest point. This schedule repeats itself day after day after day.

Loneliness has no boundaries, no rules, no codes, no principles, no regulations, no limits, no design, no supervision, no respect, and no pity. The only person who understands my pain of loneliness is someone who has lost his or her spouse.

Chapter 5

The Words I Love You

Margie and I were married for 20,373 days. I probably told her, "I love you" about two hundred thousand times, but that wasn't enough. I wish I had told her twice that many times. "I love you" is a well-known phrase, but when two hearts care, the words have a special meaning. We could speak to each other without saying a word. There was a silence of love, which only we could hear. I'm not sure about the quote, "Love makes the world go round." However, I do know love makes the ride worthwhile. Love is love. When life is good to you and you're enjoying your marriage, it is wonderful. But when one dies,

The greater the love,
> *The greater the pain.*

I cannot deny Margie's death. I must accept the fact that she is dead and I'll never see her on earth again. That is the human bad news. The divine good news is, one day I'll see her spiritual soul in heaven. At this heavenly meeting, there will be no human feelings or relationships, but we will know that the other is there. I'm learning to grieve and live simultaneously. Margie's love will remain a part of me until I die. The memory of her charms my heart and gives warmth to my soul. Love never dies.

The healing process comes during the months and months of grieving. The months of ups and downs contribute toward the final goal of being able to live without Margie. It takes physical and mental distress, it takes sadness, and it takes time to get to this attitude. Healing comes slowly. I have been patient, and I have allowed grief to chart the journey to recovery.

Whimpering and Whining to God

September 20, 2012 (four months after D-day)

I have been whimpering and whining to God about my loneliness and the pain of missing her. This morning at about five o'clock, I was asleep when God asked me, "Do you want her back like she was?"

I said *no* so loud it woke me up.

As I thought about me as a human and God as Lord, I realized God was trying to help me understand that He had mercy on Margie when He called her home. That was a great message and an eye-opening experience from God. It made me look at myself and be thankful.

Even if God was going to send her back to me, I did not want her in the pain and suffering she had gone through the past few years and especially the last six months of her life. I love her too much to be as selfish and self-centered as to ask God to return her to me.

Each day God opens my memory of the past and allows me to enjoy the rewards of our life. Each memory experience empowers me to take the next step past the grief marker. Each step forward gives me strength and determination to continue life and to surrender the human body of my spouse but hold on to the spiritual side. Each day I move closer to my own survival landmark.

I hope I never get to a point where I do not remember Margie. I want to remember the good and the bad of my entire lifetime. That way I can appreciate and praise the Lord for all the many things He has done for me.

The Pain, Fourteen Months after D-day

Tuesday, July 23, 2013

I still have strong emotional feelings for Margie fourteen months after her death. The landscape is different, but my love for Margie remains in my heart. This experience has shown me how powerful and loving God is and how small I am. I hope to gain wisdom, knowledge, stability, understanding, and strength through this encounter.

When God created mankind, He injected in each of us the ability to bear pain and sorrow from a loss. Every person will face grief in some form in his or her lifetime. The pain from each loss will be different.

It may not be the loss of a human life. The loss may be a divorce, a job, a home, a retirement; the list can go on and on. Even things like health, eyesight, hearing, smell, and touch, are a type of loss. Everyone will experience loss. How to deal with loss and continue life is left up to each person. Without God's love and mercy, a person will go through an earthly hell. And standing on the sideline is the devil, waiting to inflict as much misery, suffering, and pain as he can.

My anguish and grief could have wrecked my life if I had not allowed God to put His arms around me and comfort me. God expects me to grieve; I'm human. Margie's absence leaves a huge gap in my life, but I must face the loss and get on with living.

Saturday, July 27, 2013

Today is our wedding anniversary number fifty-seven. I went to Applebee's restaurant to celebrate. Margie loved Applebee's food. I ate her favorite dish, Oriental Chicken Salad. As I sat there and remembered our marriage, our love for each other, our good times, and our bad times … I cried a little, I laughed a little and I prayed a little. I thank

God for giving me Margie as a lifetime partner. You'd think that after being with a person for fifty-five years, it wouldn't be a big deal when God says it is time to give her up. Well, let me tell you, I'm happy for Margie as I look toward heaven, but the human who was left down here on earth hurts all the way down to his bones.

My pain is not unique. This is an experience that most married couples will go through. One spouse will die before the other. Seldom do both die at the same time. The odds of both dying at the same time are approximately one in a million, and that is the accident figures not normal death. I have a better chance of being struck by lighting than Margie and I dying at the same time. The probability of being struck by lighting in America is one in three hundred thousand. The loss of a loved one is a part of a normal life.

A Loss May Produce a Gain

Rewind to 1964

I've had different losses throughout my life, they were all different and I processed them differently. Sometimes, the result of a loss has some type of gain.

About eight years into our marriage, there was a loss of my 1934 Ford, five-window coupe, with a V8 Oldsmobile engine in it. I had transmission problems, and I worked on it in our yard. Our two children, ages seven and five years old, always wanted to help. I did not want their help, but I usually got it. After a while, I'd send them in the house. They were in my way. Sometimes they had a little grease on them. My lovely wife would come out and inform me that she did not want them in the house with their greasy little bodies and did not appreciate me sending them in. This happened several times over a six-week period. This was causing friction and irritation within our marriage.

I told the kids, "We need to be sweeter to Mama because when Mama ain't happy, ain't nobody happy."

I finally completed rebuilding the transmission and got the car back on the road. It was a sharp car. The body of the car had been taken down to the metal and then covered with copper fiberglass. It shined like a new penny. It had been chopped and channeled and set low on the ground. It had big tires and a powerful chromed engine.

About two months later, I came home from work, and my car was not in the yard. My wife told me she had sold my car to a guy in Orlando, Florida, and it was gone for good. I could feel the hair on the back of my neck rise up, and the heat from the pit of my stomach was rushing to my face. I could not believe this. I loved that car. It was mine. She had waited for me to fix the transmission so it could be driven, and then she sold it. She had sold the other love in my life. She did not have the right to do that. Just because the kids and I tracked a little grease in the house didn't give her the right to do something like this. Or did it?

Over the past several months, the kids and I had irritated Mama with the dirt and grease we tracked in the house. Although the car was fixed, the kids still worked on it when I wasn't home. I was not spending those precious hours with her and the kids, and she had had enough. I was not happy, but I did not put up much of a fight. I had learned that when I kept Margie happy, our total marriage activities were at a different level. The gain from the loss of my car was peace in our home, harmony, kindness, warmth, and a loving wife. I liked that car, but up against Margie's love, the car didn't have a chance. Her love was bigger than me and the car put together. I learned an important lifetime lesson: where there is peace there is joyfulness. Our happiness was found along the marriage path, not at the end of the pathway.

From that time forward, I was the happiest when I did something for Margie that made her happy. I loved to give her gifts because each gift demonstrated the footprint of love. I will miss the opportunities of showing love to her.

Margie received a gain by her own death. She is with the Lord and is without pain and suffering, and that is gratifying to me. When Margie and I got married, we both left our comfortable homes and started out on our own. Our loss was the security and safety of our parents' home. Our gain was each other, the plans for the future, and our children to come later in life.

Margie was my link to the past. She was a major player in that period of our lives. The loss of her created a new set of circumstances. Life as I knew it has ended.

Margie and I lived as if there would always be a tomorrow. We felt that was the way to live rather than thinking tomorrow we die. We planned for marriage, for education, for the second child, for careers, for retirement, for (some) relocating, etc. We also planned for eternity. We looked to God for our eternity, for salvation, and for our final destination. Every day was a gift from God, and we appreciated it to the fullest. Nothing is worth more than today. Enjoy life now; it has an expiration date. Death put a period to our marriage and holy matrimony.

As I look back at our lives together, the moments that I really lived are the moments when I have done things in the spirit of love.

Love Cards between Spouses

September 2012 (three months after D-day)

I found about twenty valentine cards, birthday cards, love cards, and anniversary cards that Margie had given me during our marriage, and I thought I was strong enough to read the cards again. Big mistake. It has been four months since Margie's death, but that is not long enough. I was so hungry for love words from Margie that I felt a need to read some of the old cards. It took three days of crying for me to collect myself. Crying is an outlet for pain. There is nothing wrong with crying. It is okay to cry. Even Jesus wept when He went to raise Lazarus from the dead. Jesus loved Lazarus. John 11, in the Bible, tells the whole story.

Fast-forward to April 26, 2013 (eleven months after D-day)
I guess I didn't learn my lesson very well in September 2012, when I found some love cards and reread them and turned on the crying machine. Today, Friday, April 26, 2013, I found about seventy cards that Margie had hid away. Some were from her to me and others I gave her. I know what it did to me last time, last time being four months after Margie died. Today is eleven months after her death. I will read these cards because I want to relive those moments in life. I want to read what we wrote to each other on the cards.

I reread the seventy cards. It is a refreshing look into our marriage and love. It is not easy to walk through the life and the moments that the cards represent. I cry as I revisit our past. I remember the good times and the bad times of our lives. Then God reminds me of His grace, mercy, and love for Margie, and I begin to collect my feelings and emotions. This crying session only lasted three hours. Last September the crying lasted three days. I think of Margie in heaven, and I feel blessed.

Living Alone

It is lonely without Margie. There was a time in my life when I could be alone without being lonely. As a computer scientist, being able to sit for hours, for days at a time, is a perfect attitude to possess. When designing computer systems, I could think faster than I could write. Having complete silence contributes to remembering the technical logic of the design. With the death of Margie, I faced a loneliness silence that I have never faced before.

Jesus faced loneliness when He was on the cross.

Matthew 27:46, Mark 15:34 (KJV).

Jesus cried out,
'My God, My God, Why hast thou forsaken me?'

Jesus died for the sins of the world. God had to step back and let Jesus feel the total weight of sin for all mankind. I told Margie, "When you die, you'll be in heaven in a flash and God will be standing at the gates to heaven and He'll say, 'Welcome, My child.' I want you to say to Him, 'Buddy will be up shortly.'"

She did not say that when she got to heaven because she did not remember what I said. Margie went directly to heaven when she died, just like the man who was saved when Jesus was crucified. One of the men being killed, asked Jesus to remember him when Jesus came into His kingdom.

Luke 23:43 (KJV))

Jesus said to him:

43.   Verily I say unto thee, To day shalt thou be with me in paradise.

Salvation is by grace through faith, and it is immediate, whole, and complete. One day I'll see Margie in heaven, and we'll recognize each other.

Friends and Grieving

There are times when I need friends near, but there are times when I need my space and need to be left alone. Working through the grief is hard work. I get to a point where I want to wallow in my self-pity. I go back in time with Margie and I think of the things that I still want to say to her. When I departed the Rehab Center on May 16, 2012, I stepped out into the world without my lifetime love. This phase of my life has ended and another phase is about to begin.

No two people face the same kind of loss in the same way. When I'm in the depth of depression, I remind myself that this is expected in the grief process. Such depression is normal. It is a part of a good healthy grief. Everyone will go through a depression stage.

Every Life has a Story

November 16, 2012 (six months after D-day)

I'm trying to occupy my mind with thoughts outside the death envelope. I went through thirty thousand pictures that we took during fifty-five years of marriage, and I made a personal album of my wife. I titled it: *Every Life Has a Story. This Is Margie's Story in Picture Form.*

During the creation of the album, there were painful moments, but there were also joyful and loving moments. At times I would cry, and then something would make me smile. I thank God for all He's given me. Margie and I knew death would come to one of us, but we wanted to extend life for as long as possible.

Margie's picture album will be passed down to our children, then to the grandkids, and it will live for as long as it has purpose. Every life has a story.

I have noticed within myself that I'm not the same person I was a few years ago. I'm a stronger person, and I think of others and their situation more now than I ever have. My faith is more mature, and it is healthier and deeper. Working through the grief experience makes me better able to help others who face similar situations. I could not say this if I had not relied upon God to walk with me and support me during the grieving stage. I am human, and I hurt in human ways. My life will never be the same, but there are still good things left in life. With God as my Lord, I can face earthly losses.

This diary of love, affection, and pain is written with the human side of earth and with the spiritual side of heaven. When Margie died, my spiritual side said, "Hallelujah. Praise the Lord, no more suffering and pain. Thank You, Lord, for Your love and mercy."

My human side came face-to-face with the darker side of life and with the fragile, confused, and weak side of human nature. I have much love for the woman God gave me.

CHAPTER 6

The Grief Experience

The grief experience cannot be described to another human being. How does one describe the nature of one's suffering when the suffering is in the heart and soul? When Margie died I cried for days. I asked God to stand between me and the devil, because in my condition I needed God near to protect me and help me through the grieving times. There is a time for grieving and a time to get on with life. Grieving is a part of human nature. Margie's death leaves the platform of my life changed for ever. Grieving is nerve-racking, difficult, and consuming. Dealing with the death of a spouse is hard work. It takes time to deal with emotions, feelings, misery, and tension. Grieving is a process all people must go through.

I'll no longer see Margie in the Smoky Mountains or in a foreign country or by the river stream or on the mountaintops, or on the pillows of snow or on the beaches of the world or the oceans or the other places we traveled. Now I see the actual beauty of the rivers, the mountains, the country, the snow, the beaches, and the oceans God created. God blessed us with the opportunity to see these beautiful places. We visited thirty-three US states and sixteen countries.

I do not compare my loss to anyone else's loss or figure that I suffered more than anyone else. The suffering and struggles are the norm in the loss of a loved one. As I perform a self-analysis of my marriage and my life with Margie, I think of the things I said and the things I did that hurt her. I want to cry out to her, "I'm sorry." Then I think of God's love, grace, and forgiveness. If God forgives me, then I should forgive myself and get on with living. I believe my loss is part of a bigger picture that God has authorized. I wonder if my own loss experience will somehow serve a greater purpose than I currently understand, comprehend, or appreciate. I do not see the big picture, but God does.

Margie is with the Lord, and that makes me happy. I keep rewinding and replaying fifty-five years of life with her. The good times make me smile then make me cry.

We could not make life perfect because that kind of power is only held by God, but the perfect power of God gave us a life full of His love, grace, and mercy. Margie leaves me with a memory of a great love and a wonderful love affair.

Love and Faith

We say the word *love* a lot. But do we really know the meaning of the word? Each year we set aside February 14 as Valentine's Day, and we say it is for lovers to show appreciation for each other. But what is love?

These are my thoughts and observations of the word *love*.

Love is free.
Love is firm.
Love is work.
Love is desire.
Love is gentle.
Love is humble.
Love is respect.
Love is passion.
Love is reliable.
Love is emotion.

Love is affection.
Love is listening.
Love is devotion.
Love is unselfish.
Love is fondness.
Love is enduring.
Love is forgiving.
Love is enjoyment.
Love is fulfillment.
Love is dedication.
Love is tenderness.
Love is attachment.
Love is acceptance.
Love is responsible.
Love is dependable.
Love is accountable.
Love is commitment.
Love is appreciation.
Love is unconditional.
Love is belief in others.
Love is time-consuming.
Love is endurance of all things.
Love is help in achieving dreams.
Love is help in times of disappointments.
Love is giving without expecting payback.
Love is first to encourage and last to judge.
Love is a promise of security, happiness, and joy.

The awareness of loving and being loved brings a flood of warmth, comfort, and wealth to a marriage and to life that nothing else can bring. A loving heart is the beginning of a loving marriage. During my lifetime, I haven't had enough time for love and certainly no time for hate. I do not know how to measure love. I never felt the need to measure it.

Margie and I satisfied our faith in each other when we decided we could make a life together and we got married. Our faith in God was a big part of our marriage and our lives. Margie is currently in heaven reaping the rewards of her godly faith.

Faith is like love; each go hand in hand with life. They are different, yet they are the same in unique characteristics. They duplicate each other in many ways. love and faith are family members.

They relate to each as:

Something that is free.
Something that is loyal.
Something that is endless.
Something that is hopeful.
Something that is extreme.
Something that is invisible.
Something that is limitless.
Something that is unselfish.
Something that is enjoyable.
Something that is delightful.
Something that is emotional.
Something that is acceptable.
Something that is undeniable.
Something that is dependable.
Something that is responsible.
Something that is trustworthy.
Something that is unrestricted.
Something that is immeasurable.
Something that is hard to explain.
Something that is without payment.
Something that implies a connection.
Something that is without conditions.
Something that indicates an attachment.
Something that you have to be urged to accept.

Something that you have to step out of your comfort
zone to experience.

Love and faith are two of the many wonderful commodities that God
gave mankind. I practice love and faith every day. I do not have to hear,
touch, smell, see, or taste a thing to believe in it and accept it as true.

I believe in rain, even in a drought.
I believe in sight, even with closed eyes.
I believe in taste, even when not eating.
I believe in love, even when not loveable.
I believe in stars, even when it's daylight.
I believe in hearing, even when in silence.
I believe in sun, even when it's not shining.
I believe in wind, even when it's not blowing.
I believe in God, even when He's not speaking.
I believe in touch, even when not being hugged.
I believe in oxygen, even when holding my breath.

Opposites Attract

It has been said that *opposites attract*. There may be some truth in that
quote. Margie and I were totally different in wants, desires, ambitions,
wishes, and personalities. There was also a gender difference. I was man,
and she was woman. I loooooooved that gender difference.

Margie liked a soft bed; I like a firm bed.
She was cold natured; I am hot natured.
She liked to shop; I do not like shopping.
I like house trim white; she liked dark trim.
I like Western movies; she liked love stories.
I like a warm shower; she liked a hot tub bath.
I like to fly at night; she liked to fly in the daytime.
I like high pillows on the bed; she liked low pillows.
I liked my clothes ironed, so Margie let me iron them.

My favorite color is blue; her favorite color was red.

She liked a maroon-colored car; I like a silver-colored car.

Margie loved seafood; I don't care much for seafood.

Margie wanted a dog; I don't want any type of animal.

I like chicken white meat; she liked chicken dark meat.

She had a pink bedspread on our bed, too girlish for me.

She liked to use the dishwasher; I'd rather wash by hand.

She loved her coffee; I love my iced tea.

House color, I like light gray; she liked a dark gray.

Margie did not like to gas up her own car; I gassed it for her.

I like the aisle seat on an airplane; she liked the window seat.

She wanted to belong to a health club; I did not want to.

I like to eat most meals at home; she liked to eat out.

I like to fly on vacation; she liked to fly and then drive.

She wanted us to dress in the same color; I didn't like that.

We couldn't agree on how many blankets to put on the bed.

She liked all-white tile on the floor; I didn't.

My favorite dessert is ice cream; her favorite was apple pie.

She liked Canoe aftershave on me; I like Obsession for Men.

In retirement, she wanted me to shave every day; I didn't.

For inside colors, I say all rooms should be the same color; she liked each room to have its own color.

Even with all these diversities, we had a love blanket that covered many of our issues and differences. Life is about love.

How do you fall in love with the right person? I don't know. I learned something about Margie each time we had a date. After a while I was able to understand a little bit of her personality. Her true character, disposition, and temperaments were discovered and displayed over the next fifty-five years of our marriage. I was always trying to read her, and she was always surprising me. There is one thing for sure: if you want to find the right person, let God help with the choosing.

During our first few dates, it was me, me, me as I tried to impress her with my good qualities. Later my project was to influence and persuade her that I was good husband material. As time went by, it became less of me and more of her, her, her as I fell in love with the person she was.

After marriage it became us, us, us, as we tried to make the other person happy. It wasn't too long before I took myself out of the equation, and it was all her, her, her. I was the happiest when I did something for her that made her happy, and that became my ambition in our marriage. She became the most important person in my life.

At the beginning of our marriage, sex was a big part of our life as we joined ourselves together and bonded as one. Over the years, our love for each other grew and grew. Love became the most important element within our relationship.

During the last five years of Margie's life, we did not have sex, and that was okay. It did not matter to me because my love for her was stronger than my sex drive.

Love of Simple Things

I never got tired of the simple things in our relationship. I loved to hold her hands, hug her, kiss her, touch her, talk to her, look into her eyes, smile at her, and wonder what she was thinking. Sometimes we did not actually speak to each other. Our eyes, faces, and touch said it for us. Godly love taught us earthly love.

Margie loved to hug. Each hug demonstrated our affection for each other, and we could feel the warmth of love. Most of the time, we'd hug for about fifteen to twenty seconds. Sometimes, I'd keep holding her when she was ready to release. She would smile and say, "You aggravating thing. I can't hug you too long because you want to turn it into something else."

I'd turn her loose, she'd take a few steps away, then turn around and say, "I love you."

This is one of the memories that fractures my earthly body and rips me apart. I loved hugging her.

Margie and I did not like to talk about the painful and lonely side of life. One of us was going to die before the other, and it was in God's plan for that person to be Margie. God has a reason for everything. He is in control regardless of what we say or think. God is the Commander-in-Chief, the absolute controller of everything that is in heaven and on earth. He made the universe and He is supreme in power, rank, and authority. He owns the entire universe, galaxy, and solar system. The sooner mankind realizes the truth, the sooner God will bless our world. God created us for His pleasure and enjoyment, but you wouldn't know it by the way the world treats Him.

Do you ever wonder what will bring a smile to the face of God? I do. I think God smiles when I do something that gives Him pleasure. When I obey Him and when I praise Him, I think He smiles again.

When Margie died, I became a messed-up human. I asked God to spend lots of time with me, and He did, just like an earthly father would do for his child. I'm a part of God's spiritual family, and He loves me. He placed a love barrier around me, and He became my refuge, my watchman, my caretaker, my security, my shelter, my guardian, my sanctuary, my custodian, my protector, and my safe haven. My grief pulls at me continuously. At these times I have my most intimate and innermost experience of worship with the Lord. There is no loss without pain. God will help me with my painful experiences if I share my pain with Him.

Eventually God will help me overcome the memories of the death and the loss. He'll help me relive the good times without the pain. Daily I gain more strength to live and more confidence to continue in life.

I thank God for being compassionate, understanding, and merciful to me.

After Margie and I retired, we spent most of our time together. The working years were over, and now it was time for us to enjoy our senior years. Margie was the best thing in my life. I try to remember her love and beauty. Each day I take a quiet moment to reflect on our life together. There is nothing small about life or love. Both are gifts from God. Although Margie is physically gone, her love will last a lifetime.

Eternity

Eternity. What a word. My small mind cannot describe or calculate the time frame for eternity. Eternity is forever and ever, of endless duration, everlasting, time without beginning or end. My goodness, what love God has for us. Eternity does not start when I die; it started the day I took my first breath. When I was born I began my journey to eternity. I don't get to choose when I die or how I die. I do get to choose how I live on earth and where I'm going to live in eternity.

This death experience has brought me closer to God. I need a lot of time with Him. A few weeks after Margie died, I was having a bad day and crying a lot. I held out my arms and cried to God, "I need a hug."

He put His arms around me and lifted my soul out of the darkness of pain. I have learned just how close God is and how close He has always been. He is close enough to touch. My soul is healthier from this grief experience.

I never questioned God's decision to take Margie home, and I have never said to God, "Why me?"

I would never question God. Although I miss her, I'm happy for her. I have lots of memories and a bunch of yesterdays and yesteryears. God gave me everything I have. He gave me Margie, and then He gave us love for each other. When I review the many years that we loved each other and when I become a little depressed, God lays His hands on me and whispers sweet peace to me.

What I'm Thankful for, Thanksgiving 2013

First, I thank God.

'For God so loved the world, that He gave His only begotten Son, that whosoever believeth in Him should not perish but have everlasting life.' John 3:16 (KJV)

I'm thankful for God's unconditional love, limitless grace, extensive mercy, extreme patience, universal devotion, inexhaustible passion, unrestricted forgiveness, true peacefulness, absolute power, assured security and complete understanding that He has shown me during my lifetime.

I'm thankful to God, who helps me get through the daily living without Margie.

I'm thankful for my two children and six grandchildren.

I'm thankful for my family of brothers and sisters and their families.

I'm thankful for my stepmother, who is the best stepmother in the world.

I'm thankful for the good times and the laughter our families enjoy when we are together.

I'm thankful for the wife God gave me and for allowing our partnership of love to last for almost fifty-six years.

I'm thankful for my friends who have enriched my life and given me support.

I'm thankful for their respect, patience, and unconditional love.

I'm thankful for the health of my loved ones, my family, and my friends.

I'm thankful that I have a place to sleep, food to eat, and clothes to wear.

I'm thankful for the clean air that I breathe and the clean water I drink.

I'm thankful for the benefits I enjoy, such as transportation, electricity, and air conditioning.

I'm thankful for the hospitals, doctors, and medicines that are available to me.

I'm thankful that I live in the greatest country in the world and that I am allowed the opportunities to live free and enjoy life.

I'm thankful that there are men and women who are willing to sacrifice their lives to keep this country free. They are the real heroes of our land. Without these brave souls we may not have the freedom to celebrate Thanksgiving.

I'm thankful that I have a God who loves me and a God I can trust.

Thank God for what you have.
Trust God for what you need.

The First Days in Fifty-Five Years without My Spouse

The first day (May 17, 2012) without Margie.
The first Buddy's birthday without Margie.
The first wedding anniversary without Margie.
The first Thanksgiving Day without Margie.
The first Christmas Eve without Margie.
The first Christmas Day without Margie.

The first New Year's Eve without Margie.
The first New Year's Day without Margie.
The first Margie's birthday without Margie.
The first Valentine's Day without Margie.
The first yearly holidays without Margie.
The first Mother's Day without Margie.
The first Father's Day without Margie.
The first son's birthday without Margie.
The first daughter's birthday without Margie.
The first grandchildren's birthdays without Margie.
For fifty-five years we celebrated these days together.

CHAPTER 7

Father's Day 2013

Sunday, June 16, 2013

Today is Father's Day. It has been thirteen months since D-day. God is helping me realize how blessed I am. I had Margie for fifty-five years. He wants me to enjoy the memories I have of Margie. He wants me to remember the beautiful moments that are now bigger than life. The consciousness of loving Margie and being loved back brings me joy, emotion, and warmth. God did not guarantee I would not have earthly feelings for Margie in the coming years, but He wants to get me back into the sunlight.

Rewind to May 16, 2012, D-day

When Margie died, I entered into the death tunnel of darkness. God has been trying to get me to open my eyes in the tunnel so He may adjust them to the darkness and lead me out. It was so dark in the tunnel that I didn't know my eyes were closed. I opened my eyes, and God gave me sight and directions toward the sunshine that is waiting for me at the end of this journey. Even being a Christian, I often overlook the fact that I have a God of almighty power, and I try to do things for myself. When I step back and allow my Lord to take over, things become a lot clearer. God developed solutions for situations that I thought did not have a favorable ending. He wants to help, but often I do not allow Him to interrupt what I think I can do alone. Usually, it ends up a failure because I do it the human way.

Where Did All The Years Go?

When I was a kid, an hour of time was like a day. Time passed slooooooowly. A day felt like a week. Time was not moving fast enough. At this rate I'd be an old man before I was twenty years old. Did you ever notice that the only time in our lives when we want to get old is when we are kids? I better be careful or I will end up acting like an adult that keeps screaming, "Where did all the years go?"

By our middle teens we start asking ourselves questions: Will I ever get old enough to get my driver's license? Will I ever get out of high school? Eventually I got my drivers license and I got out of school. I went into the army the same month I graduated from high school. After my tour of duty, I returned to Avon Park to begin my civilian life. So far time had been on my side. School took forever. The army got better after boot camp. Now I was back home, but I didn't remember being a teenager. Where did all the years go?

I was ready to start a future. I got a job. I got married. We had a baby. I was working, and time was passing faster now. The weeks came and went. I was in my midtwenties and trying to look to the future. I couldn't think that fast; slow down. Then the months began to come and go. Here came the second child. Wait a minute, what's happening? Who said, "We have a child starting the first grade?" Oh no! I was headed for thirty years old. Where did all the years go?

I was in my thirties, and the years were picking up speed. They were flying right past me. Hold on, I needed to make plans for the future; I didn't get to the plans when I was in my twenties. *Time*, you're moving too fast. Wait a minute, I needed more time to project the years ahead. Slow down. I hadn't accomplished our thirty-year plans yet. Where did all the years go?

Lookout, I was headed for my forties. Who said that? What do you mean we have a child graduating from high school? It was like yesterday that he entered elementary school. We had to get that boy a job. Next thing you know, he'd want a car. Time was moving too fast. Margie, we're getting older. Where did all the years go?

By my early forties, the time rate had doubled. What's going on? A few months ago I was turning forty. Time is accelerating. Hold on, I'm headed for forty-five years old to quickly. Wait a minute, there is something positive that can come out of getting older. The kids will be leaving home. Margie and I will be living alone, ha, ha. Getting older doesn't sound so bad! Where did all the years go?

My friends keep reminding me that fifty is coming. Fifty came and went in a flash. Wait, I didn't mean for time to move this quickly. It's not fair. I have been caught off-guard. It seemed like two years ago I was in my twenties. I was married and embarking on my new life with my spouse. I have a few memories of how it was back then and my dreams of things to be. Eat, work, sleep. Eat, work, sleep. I haven't had enough fun time. Where did all the years go?

Look out, middle fifties, here I come. Time, you're not going to slow me down. Margie and I are getting into the fast lane with you, and we are going to enjoy more happiness together at a higher rate of speed. Time, you might as well get used to it. Here we go! Where did all the years go?

Is it true? I'm looking at sixty years old? Is it time to retire? Retire? What will I do with all this extra time? I've been working since I was a kid. As I walk out the door for the last time, I'm saying to myself, "Where did all the years go?"

When I was in my thirties, I would see people in their fifties and think they were old. I could not imagine what it would be like to be that old. Now, I'm one of those slow-moving older people I used to see. We old people have lost our strength and mobility and gained aches and pain. We can't believe we have lived this long but we keep saying to ourselves, "Where did all the years go?"

There are things I should have done, things I should not have done, and things I am thankful to have done. Yet, there are more things I should have done and should have said. So while you can, say all the things to your family and loved ones that you want them to know. Remember one thing: life goes by quickly, and soon you'll be saying, "Where did all the years go?"

Now as I look back on our marriage and the woman I shared those years with, I thank God for letting us find each other, yet I keep saying, "Where did all the years go?"

My spouse, Margie, was a caring, sweet, lovable, and gracious person, and I love her very much. Her death forces me to look at myself and determine how I will live my remaining years without her. I lost a friend, a companion, a soul mate, a partner, a sweetheart, and a darling girlfriend. No one cares like a spouse. Every area of my life is affected by her absence. Where did all the years go?

Time has a way of moving quickly through a lifetime. I continue to wonder, "Where did all the years go? It feels like day before yesterday that I did some of these activities, but some were forty to fifty years ago. Getting old is the price we pay for living.

Adam and Eve

Rewind to the Beginning of the Human Race

Today is Sunday, February 24, 2013. It has been nine months since Margie passed away. Our church is the First Baptist Church of Brandon Florida, Pastor Tommy Green. Today Brother Green's message was about family. I thank God for the message He had for me through my pastor. I cried a lot during the family message, but I was where God wanted me to be so He could speak to my soul.

I spoke earlier about our first baby and how Margie and I did not know how to care for a child. Did you ever wonder how Adam and Eve learned to take care of their children?

Adam and Eve were living in glory land in the garden of Eden. They had everything they wanted or needed. They had daily worship and fellowship with God. They lived in a wonderland that God Himself made for them. They had eternity at their fingertips. Then enters Satan, the prince of darkness, the betrayer of mankind, the enemy of goodness, the traitor of truth, the evil spirit, the wicked one that opposes God.

Adam and Eve, the first married man and woman, sinned against God, and God turned them out of the Garden of Eden. This is the beginning of sin. This event demonstrates how powerful the devil is. He is not a little old man, dressed in red with horns, a pitchfork, and a long tail and running around the countryside. He is the one that presents everything that is sinful in a beautiful, covetous way. The devil has more power than we give him credit for.

The devil befriended Adam and Eve and smoothed over what God said they could not do. Satan has been doing this for centuries and will continue until God's judgment. Adam and Eve's sin deeply disappointed God. The Bible verses below reveal how Adam and Eve betrayed God and brought sin into the world.

Genesis 3 (KJV)
1. *Now the serpent was more subtle than any beast of the field which the Lord God had made. And he said unto the woman, Yea, hath God said, Ye shall not eat of every tree of the garden?*
2. *And the woman said unto the serpent, We may eat of the fruit of the trees of the garden:*
3. *But of the fruit of the tree which is in the midst of the garden, God hath said, Ye shall not eat of it, neither shall ye touch it, lest ye die.*
4. *And the serpent said unto the woman, Ye shall not surely die:*

5.   *For God doth know that in the day ye eat thereof, then your eyes shall be opened, and ye shall be as gods, knowing good and evil.*

6.   *And when the woman saw that the tree was good for food, and that it was pleasant to the eyes, and a tree to be desired to make one wise, she took of the fruit thereof, and did eat, and gave also unto her husband with her; and he did eat.*

7.   *And the eyes of them both were opened, and they knew that they were naked; and they sewed fig leaves together, and made themselves aprons.*

8.   *And they heard the voice of the Lord God walking in the garden in the cool of the day: and Adam and his wife hid themselves from the presence of the Lord God amongst the trees of the garden.*

9.   *And the Lord God called unto Adam, and said unto him, Where art thou?*

10.   *And he said, I heard thy voice in the garden, and I was afraid, because I was naked; and I hid myself.*

11.   *And he said, Who told thee that thou wast naked? Hast thou eaten of the tree, whereof I commanded thee that thou shouldest not eat?*

12.   *And the man said, The woman whom thou gavest to be with me, she gave me of the tree, and I did eat.*

13.   *And the Lord God said unto the woman, What is this that thou hast done? And the woman said, The serpent beguiled me, and I did eat.*

14.   *And the Lord God said unto the serpent, Because thou hast done this, thou art cursed above all cattle, and above every beast of the field; upon thy belly shalt thou go, and dust shalt thou eat all the days of thy life:*

15.   *And I will put enmity between thee and the woman, and between thy seed and her seed; it shall bruise thy head, and thou shalt bruise his heel.*

16.   *Unto the woman he said, I will greatly multiply thy sorrow and thy conception; in sorrow thou shalt bring forth children; and thy desire shall be to thy husband, and he shall rule over thee.*

17.   *And unto Adam he said, Because thou hast hearkened unto the voice of thy wife, and hast eaten of the tree, of which I commanded thee,*

> *saying, Thou shalt not eat of it: cursed is the ground for thy sake; in sorrow shalt thou eat of it all the days of thy life;*

18. *Thorns also and thistles shall it bring forth to thee; and thou shalt eat the herb of the field;*

19. *In the sweat of thy face shalt thou eat bread, till thou return unto the ground; for out of it wast thou taken: for dust thou art, and unto dust shalt thou return.*

20. *And Adam called his wife's name Eve; because she was the mother of all living.*

21. *Unto Adam also and to his wife did the Lord God make coats of skins, and clothed them.*

22. *And the Lord God said, Behold, the man is become as one of us, to know good and evil: and now, lest he put forth his hand, and take also of the tree of life, and eat, and live for ever:*

23. *Therefore the Lord God sent him forth from the garden of Eden, to till the ground from whence he was taken.*

24. *So he drove out the man; and he placed at the east of the garden of Eden Cherubims, and a flaming sword which turned every way, to keep the way of the tree of life.*

The view of the Garden of Eden depends upon where you are standing. Inside the garden, everything was amazing, incredible, enjoyable, beautiful, magic, and marvelous.

Now Adam and Eve are on the outside looking in, and things on the outside are totally different. They will experience the wrath of their sins, as will the world. Satan is still playing the game of trick or treat. He is doing the tricking and offering us a treat. The devil will continue playing us until the end of time and judgment.

Adam and Eve were the first people on earth to have children. They had three children by name—Cain, Abel, Seth—plus more sons and daughters. They did not have another human to ask about the care of a baby and how to raise and support a family.

The first child was born.

Genesis 4:1-2 (KJV)

1.   *And Adam knew Eve his wife; and she conceived, and bare Cain, and said, I have gotten a man from the Lord.*

2.   *And she again bare his brother Abel. And Abel was a keeper of the sheep, but Cain was a tiller of the ground.*

Genesis 5:4 (KJV)

4.   *And the days of Adam after he had begotten Seth were eight hundred years: and he begat sons and daughters:*

God created and sanctioned marriage to be between a man and a woman. This is not a marriage suggestion from God. It is a demand that carries the authority of enforcement. God established the first marriage as an example of how He wanted generations to follow. God said, "This marriage is man and woman, Adam and Eve." He didn't say Adam and Steve. He said Adam and Eve. He didn't say Eve and Evon. Adam and Eve. Man and woman.

My Eve was Margie. I look back at our marriage, and I see much love. I also see much love that God gave us daily. Now God is helping me accept the death of Margie.

God placed mankind above all the other creatures of the world, but most of the time we do not act as if we are the smartest of God's creations.

Kindred Hospital Stay

Fast-forward to December 2011–March 2012
Margie was in the Brandon hospital, then rehab, then back to the Brandon hospital, then Kindred Hospital, then Brandon Rehab Center,

then her final stop, heaven. The Kindred Hospital is between Tampa and St. Petersburg. She was there for seventy-six days. I went every day that I was allowed to go. I'd arrive at the hospital between 9:00 and 10:00 a.m. One day one of the doctors at the hospital said, "I can tell you really love your wife."

And I said to him, "Why would you think that?"

He said, "Because you are here early in the morning and we are still feeding her or giving her a bath or giving her medicines or cleaning her room and visiting hours don't start until two o'clock."

I said to him, "You are right; I love that woman a lot."

I continued the same routine of spending as much time with her as possible.

Margie and Heaven

Margie is in heaven, but she is not looking down on me. I do not believe that God will allow saved people to look into hell or back to earth after they die. I believe it would make a Christian sad to see people in hell in agony, suffering, misery, torment, and pain. Although they are in hell because they rejected Jesus Christ as their Savior, it's still hard for my earthly brain to believe God would let His children look into hell. Some people like to think their moms are looking down on them and can protect them in some way or warn them of danger. I don't believe that, but if it makes that person a better person for thinking that, I let it be.

As earthly humans, I believe we would disappoint the heavenly souls if they could see us. When souls are in hell, I believe they can see heaven and earth. I believe that is part of a lost person's punishment, being able to see both places.

Luke 16:19-31 (KJV)

19. *There was a certain rich man, which was clothed in purple and fine linen, and fared sumptuously every day:*

20. *And there was a certain beggar named Lazarus, which was laid at his gate, full of sores,*

21. *And desiring to be fed with the crumbs which fell from the rich man's table: moreover the dogs came and licked his sores.*

22. *And it came to pass, that the beggar died, and was carried by the angels into Abraham's bosom: the rich man also died, and was buried;*

23. *And in hell he lift up his eyes, being in torments, and seeth Abraham afar off, and Lazarus in his bosom.*

24. *And he cried and said, Father Abraham, have mercy on me, and send Lazarus, that he may dip the tip of his finger in water, and cool my tongue; for I am tormented in this flame.*

25. *But Abraham said, Son, remember that thou in thy lifetime receivedst thy good things, and likewise Lazarus evil things: but now he is comforted, and thou art tormented.*

26. *And beside all this, between us and you there is a great gulf fixed: so that they which would pass from hence to you cannot; neither can they pass to us, that would come from thence.*

27. *Then he said, I pray thee therefore, father, that thou wouldest send him to my father's house:*

28. *For I have five brethren; that he may testify unto them, lest they also come into this place of torment.*

29.   *Abraham saith unto him, They have Moses and the prophets; let them hear them.*

30.   *And he said, Nay, father Abraham: but if one went unto them from the dead, they will repent.*

31.   *And he said unto him, If they hear not Moses and the prophets, neither will they be persuaded, though one rose from the dead.*

God allowed Abraham to speak from heaven to the rich man in hell to make a point. One point is that there is a great gulf fixed between heaven and hell. Souls cannot pass from one to the other. Another point is that while on earth, he had opportunities to be saved, he and his family, but they rejected Jesus Christ as Savior.

You notice that God did not allow the rich man to speak to Lazarus. Why, I don't know. Lazarus was in the bosom of Abraham. The rich man spoke to Abraham of the Old Testament, and Abraham spoke of Moses of the Old Testament. The rich man could see Lazarus and requested Lazarus to do something for him, but he did not speak directly to Lazarus.

Truth prevails,

'You choose the behavior,

                You choose the consequences.'

This comment ......

        Was True Then,
              Is True Today,
                    Will be True Tomorrow.

Mankind has a choice. We individually choose our eternity.

CHAPTER 8

Once-in-a-Lifetime Vacation

In December 1999 Margie and I took her once-in-a-lifetime vacation to Australia and New Zealand. It was a turn-of-the-century millennium journey. We departed Los Angles on December 12, 1999, and returned on January 11, 2000. Our departure flight was United Airlines flight 815, Los Angeles to Sydney Australia. Flying time nonstop was fifteen hours.

We processed through customs in Sydney and departed for Cairns, Australia, two hours later on Ansett Australia Airlines. We arrived at our hotel twenty-one hours after departing California. About four hours later, my sister, Alma, and her husband, Robert Casanova, arrived from California. This vacation only included a foursome rather than the normal six-pack group. Usually my brother, Jimmy, and his wife, Nancy, travel with us. Jimmy was unable to be away from his business for a month.

The next day we had lunch at the Great Barrier Reef. A few days later we took a flight to Alice Springs, Australia, and then over to Ayers Rock Airport. Ayers Rock is about two hundred miles southwest of Alice Springs. Uluru, also known as Ayers Rock, is a large sandstone rock formation in the southern part of the Northern Territory, Central Australia. It's the big red rock in the middle of nowhere. Most pictures of Ayers Rock are shown as color red, but during the day and the night, the rock changes colors as the weather changes. It is usually red at dawn and at sunset. After our tour of central Australia, we returned to Sydney. We toured the Sydney area for two days.

Our tour/cruise package with Royal Caribbean Cruise Line included the above tour plus a twenty-one-day cruise. Our cruise ship was the RCCL *Legend of the Seas*.

From Sydney we sailed to Melbourne, Australia, and stayed there eighteen hours. We departed Melbourne and sailed to Hobart, Tasmania, Australia.

The Tasmanian devil is not found any where else in the world. It is only found on this island in Australia. The largest of the group is less than twenty-six pounds and no longer than thirty inches. These are dangerous little critters. Pound for pound, they deliver one of the most powerful bites in the animal world. If you present a half-inch diameter wooden stick to the Tasmanian devil, his jaws are so powerful, he'll snap the end off of it. When that kind of force in applied to human parts, the Tasmanian devil can snap arms off in one bite. He loves fingers—no challenge at all. Their lifetime is only six or seven years.

The ship celebrated Christmas Eve and Christmas Day at sea. The next big event was New Year's Eve.

We entered New Zealand Territory on December 26 via:

Fiordland National Park, NZ
+ Milford Sound
+ Doubtful Sound
+ Dusky Sound

Dunedin, NZ
Christchurch, NZ
Wellington, NZ

We left Wellington, New Zealand, for the International Dateline on December 29, 1999. This New Year's would be special. It would be the once-in-a-lifetime opportunity. We celebrated a first New Year's Eve and a second New Year's Eve.

It took us two days to sail from New Zealand to the International Dateline. It was December 31, 1999, when we arrived. We stopped west of the International Dateline and started the New Year Party. Midnight came, and we ship people are the first people in the world to celebrate the new millennium year, 2000. At daylight, January 1, 2000, the captain moved the ship east of the International Date Line and back into date December 31, 1999. We positioned the ship and settled down to start our wait for midnight December 31. We had already had one New Year's millennium party, and we were going to have another one. After the whole world celebrates the entrance of the year 2000, we ship people would be the last people in the world to celebrate the going out of 1999 and into year 2000. We had our second New Year's celebration as we ushered out the twentieth century and welcomed in the twenty-first century.

A few minutes after midnight, we headed west, back toward New Zealand. Within a few minutes, we crossed the International Dateline, and at that moment we lost a day on the calendar. On the west side of the International Dateline, it was the January 2, 2000.

We had an extra, unforeseen, and unplanned enjoyment while at the International Dateline. While stabilized and waiting for midnight, one of America's nuclear submarines spotted us dead in the water. They thought we didn't have the power to move, so they reported it to their headquarters. The sub did not try to contact our ship, and neither did the navy. But during the night CNN contacted the ship to see what was wrong. The captain recorded the conversation. The next morning he informed the passengers of the CNN call to our ship, and he played the recording to us.

The captain informed CNN that we were at the International Dateline and were celebrating the millennium new year change, and we were going to do it twice. We would be first in the world to celebrate the new century and the last in the world to celebrate entering the new century.

CNN had not foreseen or thought about someone doing this. They said, "The first day of the new year of the twenty-first century and you're celebrating New Year's twice?" They were sorry they did not have someone from CNN on the cruise; they had missed an opportunity.

CNN verified the location of our ship by way of the navy information. We were on the International Dateline. The sub had to give our exact location in case we were having problems and needed help. We were not in distress, but we appreciated the call.

We returned to our cruise cities.

Napier, NZ
Picton, NZ
Bay of Islands, NZ
Tauranga, NZ
Auckland, NZ

We went to islands in New Zealand that had never seen a cruise ship. All their necessities came to them via freight ships and barges. Some of the people were born, lived, and died without ever leaving the island. We enjoyed watching the people from these little towns and their excitement on seeing a large cruise ship in their town. One of the islands brought their city band to the pier, let the kids out of school, put a picture of our ship on the front page of their newspaper, and put up welcome banners. We were excited for their excitement. All of the islands had a sweet group of down-to-earth people.

At night we'd talk about the visits to the islands and the lovely people who were there and how happy they seemed. They had their own world

116

out there alone. Some of the islands were rather small; the ship people could have invaded the island. There were more people on the ship than the population of the town.

At the completion of the cruise, we remained in Auckland, New Zealand, for two days prior to returning to Los Angeles. The return trip took thirteen hours nonstop.

If I Had My Life to Live Over

If I had my life to live over as it equates to my spouse, my family, and my friends:

I would laugh more.
I would be more loveable.
I would still marry Margie.
I would forgive more easily.
I would say I'm sorry more.
I would visit family more often.
I would pray for more patience.
I would give Margie more hugs.
I would say, "I love you" more.
I would not sweat the small stuff.
I would talk less and listen more.
I would watch life and learn from it.
I would sit in the good living room.
I would still fall in love with Margie.
I would love more and complain less.
I would not take so many things so seriously.
I would use the good dishes for everyday eating.
I would be human and cry when it was warranted.
I would tell Margie I loved her half a million times.
I would give and receive more hugs from my family.
I would listen more carefully to what Margie was saying.
I would worry less about things that might never happen.

I would be more responsible with the care of our two kids.
I would get rid of things that weren't beautiful and useful.
I would establish a higher priority for Margie's happiness.
I would not get so busy making a living that I forget to live.
I would take every minute of life and live it fully with Margie.
I would never buy anything just because I might need it someday.

One-Year Death Anniversary

May 16, 2013

One year ago today, May 16, 2012, at 12:30 p.m. eastern time, my spouse passed away.

Today is May 16, 2013, 9:30 a.m. pacific time one year later. I'm in Arizona with family. We are reliving the life of a spouse, a mother, and a grandmother. Each of us has our own individual relationship pain to observe from the death of Margie. I relive the death zone that I was in one year ago at the rehab center when Margie and I looked into each other's eyes for the last time. I cry as I note these moments. I appreciate the years we were married and the life we had with each other. The more time God gave me with my loved one, the more time I wanted.

The pain is still visible and noticeable as I celebrate the one-year death anniversary of Margie. I am again exposed to a certain level of grief as I revisit a love of yesteryears and *The Pain from the Death of a Spouse.*

God Is the Answer

God is the answer to all of my needs. In this experience, God was my answer to my sorrow, sadness, and grief. When death came to five of my family members, God used the trustworthiness and truthfulness of His Word to guide me to relief and contentment.

Hebrews 4:16 (KJV)

> Let us therefore come boldly unto the throne of grace, that we may obtain mercy, and find grace to help in time of need.

Psalm 50:15 (KJV)

> And call upon me in the day of trouble: I will deliver thee, and thou shalt glorify me.

Psalm 48:14 (KJV)

> For this God is our God for ever and ever: he will be our guide even unto death

Psalm 105:4 (KJV)

> Seek the LORD, and his strength: seek his face evermore.

Proverbs 3:5 (KJV)

> Trust in the LORD with all thine heart; and lean not unto thine own understanding.

Philippians 4:19 (KJV)

> But my God shall supply all your need according to his riches in glory by Christ Jesus

Jeremiah 31:13b (KJV)

> For I will turn their mourning into joy, and will comfort them, and make them rejoice from their sorrow.

Matthew 11:28-30 (KJV)

> *Come unto me, all ye that labour and are heavy laden, and I will give you rest.*
>
> *[29] Take my yoke upon you, and learn of me; for I am meek and lowly in heart: and ye shall find rest unto your souls.*
>
> *[30] For my yoke is easy, and my burden is light.*

Psalm 30:5 (KJV)

> *For his anger endureth but a moment; in his favour is life: weeping may endure for a night, but joy cometh in the morning.*

I Peter 5:7 (KJV)

> *Casting all your care upon him; for he careth for you.*

God and the Bible verses were exactly what I needed to get me through the death experiences. There is physical and mental suffering with each family member's death—sister, father, mother, brother, and spouse. Margie was a part of me; her death commands the most painful distress and anguish that can be imaged. Family love is one type of love. A spouse's love is a different love altogether. I love my spouse more than I love myself.

God gave me a great blessing when He gave me Margie. I thank Him for aligning our lives so we could find each other. I did not completely show appreciation to God for all the things He provided us during our long marriage. I realize that God was the essential ingredient in our happiness, but I did not acknowledge His gifts on a daily basis. And again, we come up with the old familiar phrase: taking God, family, friends, and things … for granted.

Where There Is "Blank," Let there be "Blank"

I developed an action list that will make all people have a better life, and then someone told me there was a list on the internet. I don't know what is on the Internet, but I researched each one of these myself. They're mostly common sense.

Where there is hate, let there be love.
Where there is death, let there be life.
Where there is war, let there be peace.
Where there is doubt, let there be faith.
Where there is dying, let there be living.
Where there is wrong, let there be right.
Where there is noise, let there be silence.
Where there is division, let there be unity.
Where there is spite, let there be kindness.
Where there is darkness, let there be light.
Where there is blindness, let there be sight.
Where there is mystery, let there be clarity.
Where there is difficulty, let there be hope.
Where there is criticism, let there be praise.
Where there is sorrow, let there be comfort.
Where there is losing, let there be winning.
Where there is sickness, let there be health.
Where there is crying, let there be laughter.
Where there is dislike, let there be affection.
Where there is ridicule, let there be respect.
Where there is persecution, let there be help.
Where there is planting, let there be reaping.
Where there is receiving, let there be giving.
Where there is grief, let there be celebration.
Where there is fault, let there be forgiveness.
Where there is injustice, let there be fairness.
Where there is bondage, let there be freedom.
Where there is weakness, let there be strength.

Where there is sadness, let there be happiness.
Where there is waste, let there be preservation.
Where there is punishment, let there be pardon.
Where there is mourning, let there be rejoicing.
Where there is complaint, let there be listening.
Where there is sympathy, let there be tenderness.
Where there is rejection, let there be acceptance.
Where there is ignorance, let there be knowledge.
Where there is prejudice, let there be impartiality.
Where there is avoidance, let there be participation.
Where there is wickedness, let there be righteousness.
Where there is discrimination, let there be encouragement.

Car and Church

Rewind to a Sunday in 1990, Torrance, California

Margie and I got dressed to go to church. We walked out to the garage and got in her car. I turned the car key, and nothing happened. The motor did not turn over. It is always a surprise when the car doesn't start. I turned the key about seven or eight more times (like that was going to make a difference), but the battery was dead. I waited about thirty seconds and tried it again; not even a grunt from the car.

I said, "Thank You, Lord."

Margie looked at me sort of funny and said, "Why in the world would you say that? The car didn't start."

I said, "Because we are home. The car is in the garage. We're not sitting in some parking lot with a dead battery. All we have to do is get out of your car and get in my car. Let's do it; I'll fix your car later."

I was thankful we were not stranded somewhere, praise the Lord. God gives us heaven's blessings as well as our human toys. Sometimes the toys have a problem.

CHAPTER 9

Progression of Sickness

Stages of my Declining Spouse (11/23/2011 - 5/22/2012)

These are the actual notes that I sent to family and friends during Margie's six-month hospital and rehab stays. They will present a view into Margie's medical conditions during this time period.

November 23, 2011

Margie was admitted to the Brandon Regional Hospital today by her infectious disease doctor because of her recent Pseudomonas attack. The doctors will attempt to hammer this assault into submission by increasing the strength of her medicines. We're hoping she will be home in 10 to 12 days.

December 7, 2011

Margie has taken a turn for the worst. She was in the hospital for 8 days, and then sent to the rehab center. She has been there for 6 days, but last night she started coughing and not able to breathe. That condition lasted most of the night. This morning she called and told me she was very sick.

I called her Pulmonary (lung) doctor and got an appointment for this morning. When he examined her he sent her directly to the Hospital ER because he thought she had pneumonia and ER says it is Pneumonia. Our great concern is her having Pseudomonas and Pneumonia at the same time. That combination is not good. Her Infectious Disease doctor and her Pulmonary doctor are working together to find a solution.

When I left the hospital at 10 PM Margie was still in the ER and they were going to keep her there for more meds, via IV and by mouth.

December 15, 2011

Today we got the news that the Pseudomonas test contained some good news. When Margie was in the hospital the first time (Nov. 23, 2011), the doctors attacked the infection pretty aggressively. That was a good thing because when she got pneumonia they did not know if they had killed this round of the Pseudomonas infection. When she was put back in the hospital the second time, the Infectious Disease doctors really increased the strength of her meds and IVs. Margie had 3 different doctors. One of them told me that she was getting the strongest medicines that the Law would allow them to give to a human.

Thank you for your prayers. God and the medicines have her felling better. God did not need anyone or anything but He wanted to see how faithful we are when in need and who we look to as the great Physician.

Tonight Margie will be moved to another Hospital between Tampa and Saint Petersburg. It is a Rehab Hospital. Hospital doctors on staff around the clock and out side doctors can visit their patients, if they want. Margie will be placed in Isolation because Pseudomonas is contagious. No touching her unless you are wearing Gloves. No going into her room unless you are wearing a hospital supplied gown and mask. We'll see what is in store for her in the coming weeks.

Margie has not been home since Nov. 23, continue to pray for us.

December 27, 2011

Margie was doing good Christmas day and yesterday. Today when I got to the hospital she did not know where she was nor what was going on around her. She was breathing hard and pain in her lower chest and down through her stomach.

Margie has taken so much medicine via pills and IVs that it has affected other parts of her body. Today one of the doctors said that Margie should have only been on some of the medicines for 10 days and then taken off but they had to give them to her for a longer period because they were trying to save her life. That's what happens if you get Pseudomonas and Pneumonia at the same time. The hospital wants to do a Brain Scan Wednesday. We'll see what happens after several doctors talk tonight.

December 28, 2011
It's amazing how God looks out for His children. I did not know what God would do over night to make Margie feel better. Our son Ed is here to visit his mom. When we arrived at the hospital about 9 AM Margie was sitting up and waiting for us. She is still having a few problems but ready to see her son.

I believe it will be several days before she is back to where she was Sunday. Some of the medicines Margie takes causes additional medical problems but the hospital is trying to handle the side effects.

January 3, 2012
Margie is still in the Hospital. This starts her 40th Day away from home and in some type medical facility. The doctors are still giving her heavy doses of antibacterial drugs. She should have been takes off some of these medicines three weeks ago.

As some of you may know, when you're on strong antibacterial drugs for long periods of time the body starts generating its own way of throwing the medicines off because it does not want anymore.

So the body discharges the drugs via the Kidney, the Bladder and through the skin and any other way that it can. Margie has been in this stage for about 3 weeks. She continues to be in Isolation. No going into her room unless you're wearing a hospital supplied gown, gloves and mask.

January 5, 1012
Margie had to be transferred to another Hospital today for a problem she has been fighting for several days. The other Hospital did a procedure on her and she returned to her assigned Hospital about 3 PM this afternoon.

I talked to the Nurse Supervisor at 4:30 PM and she said Margie is resting and they would have more information tomorrow after her doctors review the results of the procedure and instructions from the hospital that she went to today.

Word of mouth is that Margie did well and the procedure was a success but we must wait for the full report.

January 9, 2012
It is difficult for me to write about Margie's condition when there is no good news.

Without a lot of explanation.... Margie is in worst shape now than anytime since being admitted to the hospital Nov. 23, 46 days ago.

I was going to see Margie almost everyday until last Tuesday when I was so sick that I had to go to the doctor. By Friday I was very sick, so I went to a different doctor. Dr. Axel, Margie's pulmonary doctor, then an x-ray. Today Monday (01/09/12) Dr. Axel said I have a Bacterial Infection and Pneumonia. He wanted to put me in the hospital, but him knowing the sickness of Margie he allowed me to beg off and stay home. Then he said, NO visiting Margie period (.). Today a week ago was the last time I saw Margie. It breaks my heart. God please help us. You guys pray for us.

January 27, 2012
(Side-note) The below note is an apologize to God for the human's lack of faith blunder

This update is a little long because I have a few confessions.

I have been sick for 3 weeks and not able to visit Margie. We talk on the phone when she feels like it. I talked to her on Monday 1/23/12 and she sounded good and I thought she was on her way back to health. I went to visit her on Tuesday 1/24/12 and I was shocked at the way she looked and how she felt, she was very sick. I returned to the Hospital on Wednesday and the nursing staff said, Because of Margie's turn for the worst she needed to go for several specialized test to determine her most recent sickness and problems. That will be done in the next few days.

Wednesday night I went to prayer meeting at our church. I talked and prayed with our church Pastor, Rev. Tommy Green, and our Adult Ministries Pastor, Rev. David Durham about Margie and her sickness.

Margie is sick-sick and not getting well. My prayers are not being answered the way I want them to be. God knows what He is doing but I don't see the big picture. I had a bad night trying to sleeping.

Thursday morning I cried and prayed for about 2 hours just me and God alone in the house. I have been selfish with my wants and my prayers.

Margie and I have been married for 55 years and I'm very much in love with her. She has been very sick and in the Hospital 64 days. I have been praying for her every day. But you know, I have been praying for God to get her well and return her to me. Although I Prayed,

'God Your WILL be done'.

I wanted God's WILL to be done if it agreed with my WILL. I was selfish with my wants. It was hard for me to visualize life without Margie.

It disturbed me that I trusted God for other things but questioned Him about healing Margie and the amount of time it was taking. I became ashamed of myself and asked God to forgive me for my behavior. You know what He did?..... He forgave me. Yessss He did. Friday morning when I got out of bed, God allowed me to rise with more patience, more understanding, more trust, with a different attitude and a different outlook on life.

Today when I visited Margie it was an altogether different visit. While Margie and I talked and showed our love for each other there was a third person in our triangle of love and fellowship?

January 31, 2012
I visited Margie today, she is better today than she was Friday, Saturday and Sunday. I talked to the Hospital coordinator, Margie's case manager and the nurses to see what's happening to Margie.

The tests that they did last Wednesday did not show any additional disease or problems. One item was brought to light and it involved her trying to take in fluids by mouth. She is still on the IVs and a small amount of liquid foods. They started giving her ice chips but every time they did she started coughing and choking. The problem, the ice turned to water then tried to go down the wind pipe, that's been the problem for several days. Solution: she gets nothing that is as thin as water. Everything by mouth has been thickening up, like broth and etc...The thick stuff goes down slower and does not get into the wind pipe as easy. They want to stop the ice chips.

This morning Margie took in 4 ounces of thick stuff and then she demanded ice chips because the ice chips feel good on the tongue. The nurse did not want to give them to her but ended up letting her have them anyway. Margie sucked the ice, and then grabbed the vacuum tube to get the water out of the wind pipe. I think she will get the message that the ice is not a good idea after a few more tries. I don't bug her about what she wants. I only explain what she is doing to herself. We're still trying to get a little food into her stomach.

The doctor said she was depressed. I can understand that. She has been through a lot.

February 13, 2012
Margie is still in the Kindred Hospital.

She had a Feeding Tube placed in her stomach Friday (2/3/12) so the hospital could feed her better food products directly into the stomach. It seems to be working better than the IV method. She is trying to take a little liquid by mouth.

I'm afraid for Margie's weak condition. She seems to be getting flu like virus, along with some other lung problems.

She is still in isolation and detached from other patients. No touching her unless wearing Gloves. No going in her room unless wearing a gown and mask.

February 16, 2012
Let me update you on the way things are going with Margie as Medicare sees it. When Margie first went into the Brandon Hospital, the day after Thanksgiving, she was there 8 days and Medicare said she has reached a certain level so she must be move to Rehab. Margie's doctors requested Medicare give them 3 to 4 more days and they would send her home. Medicare said no, so she moved to rehab. Six days in the Rehab facility and she had Pneumonia.

Back to ER and into the Brandon hospital. She was taking extra-extra strong medicines to fight the Pseudomonas and Pneumonia sickness. In 6 days here comes Medicare. 'We must move her out of the hospital and back to rehab'. Margie's doctors went right through the roof but there was nothing they could do. Medicare finally agreed to move her to another hospital between Tampa and Saint Petersburg. It is a hospital that has No ER and No Operating Room. So she went to the Kindred Hospital.

Margie is running out of Medicare hospital days, yesterday 2/15/12 Medicare said it's time to move from this hospital to a Rehab center. They do not care if she can stand up or help herself. It's time to move. Yesterday and today she tried to stand up and with help she took 3 steps and had to sit down. She will be moving soon because Medicare said 'move or Medicare will stop paying.'

She is better than she was 2 weeks ago but not well enough to take care of herself. I fussed to the CEO of the hospital, the case manager and everyone else but it did no good. When Medicare says they will stop paying, the facility will move you somewhere. This is the eighty-third day that Margie has been under medical care and away from home.

February 17, 2012

I don't know what comes next with Margie. She is trying to get stronger and be a good patient but she is so weak and not body-strong. It's hard for me to see her with so much sickness and very little body strength.

A few days ago I really got messed up. Margie started crying and begging to go home. Oh, my goodness. It is hard to keep telling her just a little longer.

Thursday (2/16) the hospital said they were discussing the transfer of Margie to rehab as soon as all the doctors gave their approval. The hospital Primary doctor said okay. Two more doctors have to approve the move.

Today, Friday 2/17, Margie's Infectious Disease doctor said she has some type of Blood Infection which will need treatment and they may have to remove her 'port' and install a new one. The 'port' is what they use to do IV's into her blood. Please pray for both of us, Margie is so depressed. I don't know how to lift her spirits. Thank you for your prayers.

February 20, 2012

Since my last update, I have visited Margie Saturday, Sunday and Monday. She wants me to come back tomorrow. I'm still getting over my flu like pneumonia. The doctor told me to only visit 3 times a week sometimes 4 if conditions required it, but not everyday. It is hard for me to stay away from her. I have to be very careful, I'm still sickly and this hospital has some really sick people.

The blood infection is being treated with IV type medicines. The doctor is trying this method before trying something more difficult and risky. She is still very weak. The hospital started getting her into a chair last Saturday and increase the sitting time every couple of days. Starting with 1 hour and going up 20 minutes until she can sit for a couple of hours.

February 25, 2012

As most of you know, Margie has a 'PORT' in her right shoulder which was installed when she had Cancer. It has been very useful to get medicines into her blood stream via the 'PORT'. The 'PORT' and her blood have become infected and the doctor has tried to solve the problem with medicines. The drugs are not fixing the problem.

Monday 2/27, about noon time she will have the 'PORT' removed. If no infection has developed around the 'PORT' and the 'port' tubing areas the doctor will install a new one. This will take place in one of the Tampa Hospitals. After recovery she will be returned to Kindred Hospital. I'll tell you, it is not easy seeing your spouse so sick for so long..... 94 days and counting. Remember Margie with a prayer about noon on Monday.

March 2, 2012

Margie moved from Kindred Hospital to the Brandon Health and Rehab Center Wednesday night. She had to leave the hospital environment because Medicare will not allow a person to stay more than 90 days in the hospital. When Margie first went into the hospital, I thought,

'90 days is a long hospital stay, Margie will be well and back home a long time before running out of hospital days.' That did not happen in Margie's case; she did run out of hospital days.

The rehab center will start to feed Margie small amounts of soft food by mouth and decrease the amount of food she gets through the feeding tube in her stomach. They took her to the exercise room today, she did a little bit of moving.

I'll keep you informed of her progress.

March 14, 2012
Today we got bad news. Margie's condition has taken a turn for the worst. We were hoping she'd be coming home in a couple of weeks. When she went from a hospital isolated clean environment to a rehab center, there were different types of germs floating around and they jumped all over her. I am afraid for her.

Margie's Pseudomonas is back, along with another bacterial infection that is attacking her lungs. She also has a bladder and kidney infection. Now we are back to lots of antibiotic medicines. We do not know how bad the Pseudomonas is. The Rehab Center does not have the equipment to perform the correct testing.

If we had known she would be getting sicker, we may have thought about bring her home from the hospital and skipping the Rehab. But she really needed to be stronger because I cannot lift her and take her to the bathroom and do the other things that would be required for her if she was home. Plus she would have to be taken to different doctors everyday to get her medicines through the IVs.

Thank you for being so concerned.

March 21, 2012
Margie was moved from the hospital to the Brandon Health and Rehab Center about 3 weeks ago. She is doing okay but still having problems

132

with different parts of her body and she continues with some of the same sicknesses she had in the hospital.

She is trying to do exercises for strength so she can get out of rehab and come home. If we can get her home, we'll be going to the doctors every day because her sickness will not be over. But at least we will be seeing doctors that are specialist in their medical field. Almost anything is better than the 119 days we have just gone through. We'll wait upon the Lord.

We thank God for the strength he gave both of us to survive this period.

March 28, 2012
Margie is really taking her Rehab exercise program seriously. She is trying to do 2 sections a day and she is getting stronger. That will help her get home sooner; however, the Rehab center will not let her go to her outside doctors for her immune system medicines. Rehab will not take the responsibility of outside drugs. I can understand that.

Margie's infectious disease doctor is worried about her Pseudomonas when she doesn't have her immune system medicine. Rehab sent her to see the infectious disease doctor today for an analysis of her condition. But no outside drugs from her cancer doctor or infectious disease doctor while in Rehab care.

At some point we will have to weight one illness against the others and make a decision. We'll see what happens over the next few days.

April 4, 2012
I'm sorry that I have not been updating you every few days about Margie's progress. I have been going back and forth to be with Margie and I'm having a hard time keeping the pace that I've set for myself.

Margie was in the hospital for 90 days and is now in Rehab and will be there for several more weeks. She has been in the hospital or rehab for almost 5 months. She is still very weak but getting stronger. Margie takes a lot of medicines and the doctors keep adding more.

I'll give you more details on the next note. Thank you for being such good friends.

April 28, 2012
Margie is still in the Rehab Center and still really sick. She will not be able to go home until she gets off some of the IV medicines. A couple of her outside doctors want her out as soon as we can because they need to address some of her problems. They are the specialists and they know her history. Of course we know that if we hang around rehab until her Medicare runs out, Medicare will kick her to the curb in a flash.

When we first went into rehab they would not let me take her to an outside doctor but when she got worse with certain conditions, they changed their minds and they started provided the transportation for her to see her regular doctors. Last week, Rehab took Margie to her infectious disease doctor because of her recent Lung problems. She coughs constantly. The doctor gave her a Whooping Cough shot. He's not sure that she has whooping cough, it sounds like it, but it could be a combination of Bronchitis, Asthma, and COPD causing a Cough. However, if it is whooping cough, it is very contagious and can be distributed to others by a cough or a sneeze. The Tampa Bay area is having a Whooping Cough problem right now.

May 8, 2012
Sorry for being late with my update. We have been hoping for better health and a go-home date to be assigned. We were trying to come home Saturday, May 5 but Margie was not well enough so the discharge was cancelled.

Margie got better during the week, so Monday May 5, we talked the doctor into letting us come home this coming Monday May 14. Then Monday night May 5 Margie could not breathe so when I went in Tuesday, there were several people working on her. The doctor was in Sun City with other patients but it was serious enough that she came to Brandon to assist with Margie.

The discharge scheduled for Monday May 14 was cancelled. Now we do not have a new go-home date. After 5 1/2 months of being in the hospital and rehab, I'm not sure there will be a go-home day.

I have totally turned it over to God, I thought I had already done that months ago but I was still trying to influence the Lord with my wishes. Now I'll accept anything God provides. That should have been my attitude from the beginning. I love her so much I want her healed and home with me. We call that selfishness, us humans seems to have an over dose of that.

Thank you for your prayers and concerns.

May 14, 2012

For the last few days, Margie has been going in and out of a coma. She went into the coma and no one could bring her back to a wake-state. I sat in a chair next to her bed and cried and prayed all night long. The rehab personnel brought a bed into the room but the bed was too far from Margie. I wanted to be close to her and touch her.

May 15, 2012

Tuesday morning I went home to take a bath and get our daughter Wendy and return to the rehab center. We stayed all day with Margie. She was in a coma all day. She had nothing to eat or drink.

I took Wendy home and I returned to the rehab to stay with Margie Tuesday night. At 10 PM I decided to go home and get some rest. I felt guilty about leaving my sweetheart alone but I needed rest. I said to God,

'Lord, if this is the end, I haven't said my final good bye to Margie'.

May 16, 2012

About 9:30 AM, Wendy and I walked into Margie's rehab-room and she was in a wheel chair and as bright as day and looked beautiful. The thought that came to my mind was what I said to God last night, 'I have not said my final good bye'. God performed a miracle and gave me time with my sweetheart to say good bye. I took the opportunity to hug and kiss her and talk to her. The entire rehab staff was shocked at what God had done. They could not believe Margie was awake.

About 10:30 AM Margie was back in a coma. God had fulfilled my last night prayer request and had given me extra time with her. Wendy and I stayed with her holding her hand, crying and praying. Two hours later she was with the Lord. Wednesday May 16, 2012, 12:30 PM.

May 22, 2012

We had a great Funeral yesterday, Monday 5/21/12. Margie had already been in Heaven and with Jesus for 5 days, having joy and waiting for the rest of us. We earthly Christians rejoiced with the assurance of a heavenly home for Margie and for all Christians but we felt a great loss when Margie left 5 days ago. Pray for me.

Chapter 10

Valentine's Day 2014

Fifty-five Years of Valentines

Three days before Valentine's Day 2014, I sent this note to some of my friends.

> Hello,
>
> I'm only sending this to my guy friends to help you select a gift that shows your love for your spouse. Since I don't participate in Valentine's Day anymore, I'm offering suggestions. If you want to see a side of your wife that you've never seen before, buy her a bathroom scale for Valentine's Day.
>
> Maybe you shouldn't tell her about my suggestion; just surprise her. Yes, I'm smiling as I write this.
>
> I've finished the draft of my book, and I have a few minutes to help my friends.
>
> Have a great Valentine's Day.
>
> Buddy

I did this to my wife once. I gave her a bathroom scale for Valentine's Day. Now wait a minute—don't judge and sentence me so quickly.

The date was late January 1987. Margie told me that her bathroom scale was broken, so I took notice and just filed the information away.

Then I thought, *Valentine's Day is coming. I'm not going to let this opportunity get away. I don't get many openings like this one. Oh! This is going to be good.*

Valentine's Day arrived. I got up to dress for work, and I tossed her old bathroom scale in the garbage and replaced it with a pretty new one.

I was thinking, *This should make her happy. She has a need, and I am satisfying it.*

About an hour later Margie called me at work and said, "What's this in my bathroom?"

I said, "I know it is beautiful and overwhelming but you should still be able to recognize it. It's a bathroom scale."

She said, "I know that, but what is it for?"

I said, "It's for weighing yourself."

She said, "But what is it for?"

I could tell by the tone of her voice that she was getting pretty irritated. I said, "Today is Valentine's Day; it's your Valentine present."

She said, "It better not be."

We said good-bye and hung up.

About eleven that morning I had a florist deliver a dozen red roses and a pound of See's Candy to her. When the florist arrived, Margie was in a meeting and was unable to receive her items. She worked in a secure area, and the florist could only get to the front door. Security called one of the secretaries to come and get the items and place them in Margie's office.

The secretary happened to be a friend of ours by the name was Susan. Susan later explained to me the events of the flower-candy operation.

As Margie was returning to her office she met Susan in the hallway caring the items. Margie said, "Those are really beautiful red roses."

Susan said, "They are beautiful, and there's also a pound of See's Candy." Then four seconds elapsed. Susan said, "But they are not mine, Margie." Another four seconds elapsed. Susan said, "They belong to you." Susan said she tried to drag out the suspicious mind of Margie and enjoy the moment.
Margie was thinking, *Susan's husband sent her flowers and candy, and I got a bathroom scale?*

Later we all laughed about it together.

You know what Margie did? She called the florist to see what day I had ordered the flowers and candy. *They were ordered the day before Valentine's Day.*

Later in the day Margie called me. When I answered the phone and she knew it was my voice, she said three words: "I love you." Then she hung up.

This was one of fifty-five Valentine days. I love to remember these special occasions in our marriage. Sometimes I smile; sometimes I cry.

The End-of-Life Decisions

Years ago Margie and I decided that the end-of-life conversation should take place before it was needed. We talked about wants and desires. Funeral arrangements, where to have the funeral, type of flowers, open casket, closed casket, donating body parts, cremation or burial plot, do not resuscitate, do resuscitate, burial plans, etc. We both prepared a living will and a health care power of attorney describing desires and medical treatments. We each placed the other as number one to make decisions for the other spouse.

We both agreed that:

- o we would die, probably separately,
- o we would have an end-of-life moment of truth,
- o we would have a funeral service,
- o we would have family sadness,
- o we would have extreme grief when one died,
- o we would be unhappy without the spouse's love,
- o we would see each other again in heaven,
- o we would like to extend life with each other for as long as possible.

The End of the Diary

Eighteen Months after D-day

As I end my eighteen months of grief record-keeping, I have many things to be thankful for, like the prayers, the love, the understanding, the empathy, the kindness, and the patience that loved ones and friends have shown me since the death of my spouse. I say thank you to all of them.

The end of the diary does not mean that I have stopped the living journey; it means I have stopped the written record of my journey.

When I started the grief process, I hated grief because it produced such extreme pain. Once I realized it was necessary for me to go directly through grief to achieve a healthy grief process and to produce a positive outcome, grief and I became friends. We gained respect for the work that needed to be done to guarantee a successful bereavement period. I acquired a vision of the grief experience and became willing to work through the grief. I need to succeed in this survival course to be able to continue life without Margie.

Prior to Margie's death, I had gone through the death experience with other family members. Each death had its own beginning and end. The flow of grief for each death carried its own wave of pain. When Margie died, I was immediately dumped into the deepest part of the ocean of pain. It would have been easy to take a deep breath of the ocean of pain waters and give up. I could have become a hermit and locked myself away, but instead I looked to God for comfort, grace, and mercy. He gave me that and more.

Recovery

I expect to have a certain amount of grief for the rest of my life. I will never totally recover from my spouse's death. I will get better with time, but I will never forget Margie, and neither will I forget the pain I experienced at her death. I'm not at the end of the journey, but I have reconnected to the living part of my life. When I see Margie in heaven, my grief journey will be over. This grief experience has given me a new appreciation for life, love, and marriage.

My Six Footprints to Recovery

1. God and lots of praying.
2. I wrote a diary of grief and emotion. I included the pain, suffering, and sadness associated with the loss of my spouse. I

also included the emotional aspects of our love and passion and memories of our marriage.

3. I talked with friends who knew and loved Margie, and we discussed the good times of past years. We laughed about the things we did and enjoyed together. This action helped me advance my grieving stage to the next level.

4. I gave Margie's earthly things away, mostly clothing, within four months of her death. Her possessions held past memories that kept eating into my soul of loneliness.

5. I created a picture album of Margie's life. This granted me a unique observation of our life together. Through our account of love, romance, courtship, and emotion, I acquired a deeper love for this woman as I strolled the streets of memories with her.

6. I accepted the loving advice of two friends, Bill and Linda Clark. They noticed a vast difference in my attitude, mood, mind-set, and demeanor as they identified a New Buddy in town. He is not the Buddy they have known for thirty-eight years. They would like the Old Buddy back, but the Old Buddy will never be able to resume life as usual. The Old Buddy cannot be revived rationally, psychically, emotionally, or internally. The New Buddy may be with us for the rest of his life.

Bill and Linda suggested that I listen to a relaxation CD that they owned. They hoped I might find calmness and stress and anxiety relief by listening to it. Well, like a lot of things that people suggest to me, I said okay, but in the back of my mind I was thinking, *This is not going to do any good. The agony, torment, and misery that I'm in cannot be helped by a compact disc.*

They said, "Take it home with you and just play it. Maybe you'll hear something that may be beneficial and worthwhile."

I promised to take it home and play it, and I did. That was 623 days ago, and I have not missed one day of playing the CD since June of 2012. I received my own copy a few days later. It was by

Matthew Fallon and was called *Relaxation: Stress and Anxiety Relief.* I began to play my CD several times a day to learn the suggested relaxation methods.

Each night I go to sleep listening to my CD. Why? Because it is calming, soothing, peaceful, comforting, and relaxing.

I love my audio relaxation compact disc. Through it, I discovered a method of recovery and readjustment and the ability to manage stress.

Title of CD:	*Relaxation: Stress and Anxiety Relief*
Author of CD:	Matthew Fallon, Certified Hypnotist, Life Transformation Coach
E-mail address:	*Now@AttainYourFullPotential.com*
Phone Number:	(818) 723-4508
Website:	*www.AttainYourFullPotential.com*

These are my six steps to realization of death and recovery. I could not continue life without Margie if my only perception of life was a vision of things to come. To reestablish life and to return life to absolute, I have to live life without Margie.

Poem: Margie, the Girl Next Door

A walk through life in a poem of one-liners.
(A recap of the first sight of Margie and the last sight of Margie)

Who is that moving to our street?
    I hope it is someone really neat.

They have a daughter that I can't see,
    I wonder what she will turn out to be.

She was too young to get my attention,
    Too small a body to have dimension.

She was not pretty at twelve years old,
    Not even inviting to hold.

I looked at her and I saw a child,
    But things changed after a while.

She looked different at four years older,
    Now I see her and I want to hold her.

Who is that girl walking past our house?
    Could she be a future spouse?

It's the girl next door, my family cried,
    She's beautiful now and doesn't hide.

She is good looking and quite attractive,
    If you want her, you better be proactive.

I saw a girl I wanted to please,
    I saw a girl I wanted to squeeze.

My heart raced, and my eyes popped out,
    I wanted this girl, and there was no doubt.

Is this really the girl next door?
    I can't believe the growth years of four.

I stumbled as I ran into the street,
    She said, "Don't trip over your own feet."

I screamed, "I'd like a date, if you don't mind,"
    She said, "Your date will come when I am blind."

She pushed me aside as she went her way,
    She smiled and whispered, "Perhaps someday."

It wasn't long before I got a date,
    But maybe I was just freight.

It didn't take long for me to know,
    I loved this girl and I can't let go.

I presented myself as husband material,
    She responded as if I was cold cereal.

I told her of my qualities and position,
    She said she had no interest or mission.

"Do you think it is love?" my family asked,
    "And if you get married, will it last?"

I truly don't know how she might feel,
    I only know she makes me reel.

After we dated for about a year,
    I suggested we make it a career.

I asked her to marry me, and she said yes,
    I was thrilled to change her address.

Her father said, "You're taking my girl."
    "Yes sir, I'm making her my pearl."

I love the girl who was given to me,
    She locked my heart and kept the key.

We are both equal in every respect,
    It is my duty to love and protect.

She became a mother of two,
    And immediately had lots of things to do.

Moved to California with the kids in their teens,
    Hoping the move would satisfy my dreams.

The children grew up and soon were gone,
    We wondered if this was how the plans were drawn.

Margie found work that suited her taste,
    She didn't want her life to be a waste.

We had no yacht or fancy things,
    And neither did we have bugs, spiders, and things that sting.

We worked and played and enjoyed each other,
    And grew closer together than our own mothers.

When will the time come for us to retire?
    I'd like to do it before I expire.

What will it take besides money?
    I have my spouse who is made of honey.

We retired in Florida, where the days are sunny,
    We had forgotten the allergies and the nose so runny.

In later years when sickness came,
    We had no fault or lifestyle to blame.

The diseases came, and we saw our threat,
    God stepped in and said, "No sweat."

"You're a child of the King," He said,
    "Just remember who is the universal head?

"I will be with you until I call you home,
Then you'll be in heaven, no more to roam."

We held God's hand as we walked through sickness,
He controlled the conditions and the healing quickness.

"It's time to go," as He pointed to heaven,
"I'll meet you tomorrow about seven."

God revealed His smile as He turned to go,
Our eyes could not look at His face of glow.

When daylight came and He returned,
We knew He was taking her to a place unearned.

God looked at Margie and held out his hand,
"Do you hear the music of the angel band?"

Margie looked at me, then closed her eyes,
No more living beneath these skies.

God left with Margie, and then He looked back,
He knew my earthly days would be black.

God's Spirit returned to take care of me,
He knew my need to be set free.

She's in heaven now with no regret,
I'm so happy that we met.

God helped me through the darkness of death,
I can now take a breath.

God's Comfort Zone

I did not prepare for a life after Margie. I never gave myself permission to even consider living without her. I love this woman. But then came the sickness and then came God because He loves her too. After months and months of sickness, God reached from heaven into Margie's rehab room, touched her hand and said, "Margie, My child, you have suffered enough, come home with Me."

I'm not angry with God for taking Margie home because He is not only Margie's God—He is my God and Father also. God demonstrated His love, compassion, and mercy when He invited Margie to come live with Him. Her spirit is living in heaven. Her human aspects will remain on earth with her family and friends.

Margie's footprint remains within the composition of our two children and six grandchildren. Her footprint remains within my heart and within .....

The Pain from the Death of a Spouse.

I have found a degree of peace and hope. I may even find a degree of closure, but I'll never forget the love and the relationship. It is not easy to get on with life, but if I take my eyes off of myself and look at God, He promises to care for me until He calls me home. Until then I'll remember and feel ...... *The Pain from the Death of a Spouse.*

As I end this diary of love, loss, and pain, I'll do an array of soul searching and housekeeping. It has been a struggle to get through my battles of lost love. As I step back and review the past eighteen months, I realize that I did not travel alone on the roadways of grief. God was ahead of me, clearing the way. God allowed the human side of me to cry, to scream, to groan, to grieve, and to feel the loneliness of ... *The Pain from the Death of a Spouse.*

I hope this diary of life, love, marriage, death, and grief will help you find the strength and courage to survive ... *The Pain from the Death of a Spouse.*